COPYRIGHT PAGE

DEDICATION

To my Mum who gave me love and shelter from the cold and the dark when I was in my greatest pain...

TABLE OF CONTENTS

Stop Putting Up With Procrastination:
"Here's How You Can Easily Conquer Fear & Finally Achieve The Things You Want… *Without Pain!*"

The 20's Plenty Plan

How To Get The Life You Desire & Feel 20 Years Younger In Only 20 Minutes A Day...

ABOUT THE AUTHOR

Twenty's plenty to get you into shape physically, mentally and emotionally. I can get you the lifestyle you desire and feeling 20 years younger, in only 20 minutes a day.

Garth is qualified in coaching, neuro-linguistic programming and clinical hypnotherapy. He has been a key note speaker at events covering subjects such as Personal Safety for Women, Confidence and body language, Lifestyle, Stress management, Wellbeing and has been featured in the London Evening Standard and various other publications for getting a journalist from fat to fit in 8 weeks.

His workshops on Safety Awareness and Confident Life Skills have been implemented across a wide spectrum of organisations including Astra Zeneca, Diageo, BP, Sony, Anglo American, BAE Systems, ICI and many London advertising agencies. He has been a personal trainer, kickboxing instructor and nutritionist with a large and successful client base around Kensington, Chelsea, Mayfair,

Knightsbridge and ultimately a "Lifestyle Management" practice in Paddington.

You might have seen Garth on BBC television's Boomtown series, The Chrissy B Show or on Sky News.

He's had plenty of ups in his life, and all the associated benefits – A high-powered career, a beautiful wife, two gorgeous kids, a wonderful home, his and her cars and motorbikes, exotic holidays. Overall a very comfortable life. He's also hit the skids too – redundancy, financial disaster, divorce and despair. He knows the challenges of both ends of the spectrum. He's always been into fitness and discovered that exercise helped him to weather the stormier times, giving him the energy to take action.

Garth is his own living testimonial when it comes to reinventing yourself and finding your purpose. Some people seem to have a natural charm, confidence and people skills, but interpersonal skills can be taught and enhanced with The Lifestyle Guy.

Thank you for investing in a copy of my book "The 20's Plenty Plan".

I'd like to gift you a special audio recording that I put together ONLY for smart people like you who are willing to commit to personal development.

Step into your future and create the future that you want…

Just go this secret page on my website:

https://garthdelikan.com/book-bonus/

CHAPTER 1: The beginning

So, there it was, another forty-five minutes of blood, sweat and tears over.

I was showered, changed and sitting at the juice bar of my local gym sipping on my protein smoothie and feeling my depleted glycogen stores being filled up again as that delicious brew worked its magic and enjoying what I affectionately call the "afterbask"!

This is that glorious feeling (for me at least) when you have just finished a fabulous workout, pushing yourself hard and feeling the buzz of hot blood coursing through your veins.

This is the moment when all is well in your world, that immeasurable feeling of well-being and calm and accomplishment, which stays with you for hours afterwards.

That moment when you have "Clarity of Thought" and stress just seems to be an alien concept and has no place in your world or lifestyle.

This is my "special place" the place I discovered many years ago during my years working as a Director within one of London's largest companies

It was in this place of personal safety and power that all my best decisions were made, it was here that I was always calm, always strong and I found out that the benefits carried on far beyond the realm of the "mortal world" enhancing every aspect of my life, spirit and soul.

To me this feeling is so special and in the early days I seemed to be only able to achieve it through strenuous workouts, the feeling of a heavy weight in my grasp, the visualising of the physical and mental challenge I was just about to undertake, the strain of my sinews as they contracted against the resistance and the constant rhythm of the repetitions.

Unlike many of my workout partners over the years of which I've had many and unlike I'd like to add the majority of people who use gym facilities and only go through the motions of a workout and never ever feel the true benefits the true power to be accessed and used.

To me working out at the gym is special, you go there to workout, to increase your fitness, improve stamina, change body shape, heighten mental capacity, it's a place if you let it, where wonderful things do happen not only physically but also mentally!

It's not a place to go to if you're not serious about massive and positive change and to have a conversation about the weather or to chat incessantly in between exercises, to my mind that's wasted effort as you lose your concentration your focus and that's one of the many reasons that most people are unable to achieve not only their gym goals but also their life or work goals, lack of concentration on the job at hand and forever daydreaming about what could be instead of applying the effort here and now!

To my mind, it's like driving a car and then turning to talk to your passenger or speaking to someone on your mobile telephone, you take your mind off the task at hand and then become distracted, you may drift off course or worse still have an accident!

To me it's the shrine were I go to worship, the place were intense concentration to the exclusion of all outside influences is a prerequisite, it's a place where I can use my mental strength and tenacity to forge not only my body to the shape I wish but it's also the place where I can forge my will in the heat of an intense inner battle, me against the weights or resistance, my will forcing my body and my mind beyond it's normal boundaries, forcing myself to push past what I perceived as previously unconquerable goals.

Sometimes you must discover that what the mind sometimes believes isn't always necessarily so, it might just be stuck because you haven't made any demands on it recently and it doesn't know any better, it hasn't had to expand past it's usual preset boundaries.

"What the mind can conceive it can achieve" it is often written, but what if it's power to "conceive has been limited by limitations that either you, life or other people have given it?

Reading in between the lines, if you're a business man or woman or someone in business for yourself you can see the "secret" that's imbedded in this simple message and you don't need it spelling out, (do you?)

Of course not, it's not only the physical and mental challenge we're talking about here, it's here in the "afterbask" that you discover amazing things about yourself, when you have intense mental concentration coupled with the joy of doing something worthwhile, being true to yourself and then beating your previous personal best, lifting more weight than before, doing more reps than you thought possible pushing your mind beyond what it thought was previously possible, that's where the "magic" happens, that's where powerful changes begin to occur, that's where you discover your power.

No matter how tough the challenge or seemingly overwhelming the odds the joy and pleasure comes from the "effort" and it matters not if you succeed or not, the power comes from trying and if you surpass all expectations in the process, so much the better!

Being in that moment is an awesome feeling, one charged with electricity and joy and all feelings of fatigue simply disappear as though they were never ever there in the first place.

But it doesn't end there, does it?

That's only the beginning, only the first part of the magic!

CHAPTER 2: The Magic Journey

Wonderful and powerful things start to happen afterwards, once your blood stops pumping through your body quite so vigorously once your system starts to come down to normal, once the realisation of what you have achieved starts to come into focus and those wonderful little chemicals commonly known as endorphins start to kick in, or the "Pixie Dust" of the universe as I like to call it, what happens?

A wonderful feeling of calm descends around you, everything falls into sharp focus, the breathing is even, colours are sharper, brighter, happiness descends and transcends, the world is a beautiful place as it always has been but in this state it's like having the ability to step in between universes and see reality and situations like they truly are, there are no problems, no pressure, simply solutions and from this perspective it all seems so easy....welcome to clarity of thought, the power of the "afterbask"!

The power of the "afterbask" is immense and mustn't be underestimated for it's here that your true power, your true self, your inner you exists and is waiting to be discovered and used, the universe gives you this power for you to use and it's vital you learn how to tap into it if you want to get where you want to be.

You may already have the "route map", you may already have the "vehicle" and your journey may have started but clarity of thought coupled with the "afterbask" is your super fuel, your key to your inner universe, the route map that is everything.

There is more than one route to the "afterbask" and I will cover those different routes with you later on but for the time being if you'll be patient I'd like to stay with the physical route, there's a reason for that which isn't apparent at the moment but as this book unravels and you share my journey you will also pick up your own meanings, messages and routes to this wonderful nirvana this special place.

My journey in life has been a wonderful journey, it hasn't always gone according to plan especially in the "in between" years as I like to call them but as I recount my journey I'd like to share with you how the "afterbask" has served me throughout my entire life and bear in mind that I have only named it the "afterbask" in recent history after pondering and reflecting the many changes, some good, some not so good that have occurred in my life and yet this wonderful almost mystical force seemed to be the one constant in my life, the unknown force at the time that has always looked after me and guided my life and decisions.

My life has always seemingly been blessed, I've always been upbeat, had a positive attitude (most of the time) but even I have to remember that I'm not an android and someday I will wake up feeling not so good and someday things will not always go according to plan the key is to not focus on the "not happening" and focus on the "happening".

CHAPTER 3: Within or Without?

In the early 70s I worked in the publishing industry as what was affectionately called a "lick n stick" or paste up artist. This basically involved designing layouts and logos for various magazines before the advent of desktop publishing. All our type came to us from the printers or copy setters in galley form which were basically reams of type in column form which we cut up and made fit the various column inches, applied wax or spray glue onto the backs and then "stuck" them into place!

It was an exciting time and even then, in my early 20s I always had an inner confidence and charm and always felt special inside that somehow translated into being "extroverted" for want of a better phrase but it was that "Joi de vivre" that that helped me to sail through life and achieve things at an early age that other people seemed only to be able to aspire to.

When I look back on it now it was me being so in love with life and so filled with energy that my joy was infectious and I used to have a huge circle of friends and was always very popular. I was "centred" within myself without even knowing it, inadvertently I had unconsciously entered the world of the "afterbask" and was projecting a can do attitude even at that early age that other people seemed to pick up on and to my mind nothing seemed impossible nothing was insurmountable, I was living from "without" and living "without" was a great place to be, being and coming from "without" means that you're not shut up in your own little world and internalising and emotionalising every thing you do and feel you're not living your life "within yourself" you are living in the outside world and picking up the joy and vibrations that the world and the universe has to offer.

Living "without" translates to my mind at least to being in pure joy, no worries, no insecurities, just being the real you, and when you are the real you it's like being a huge magnet to not only the world at large but also to the universe.

Your energy and enthusiasm resonates and attracts everyone and everything you require into your life without any effort and to be honest without even trying and thinking about it.

I proved this at a time when most people were charging a fixed hourly rate which was perceived the upper ceiling rate at the time, I wanted more out of my life and decided to buy myself a motorbike at age 22 and become a mobile "freelancer" charging double the rate of the time and in some instances charging what I thought the "job was worth" not an hourly rate, "an outrageous attitude" to have, I was told time and time again by the disbelievers.

I was always professional, meticulous and courteous because I believe that good manners cost nothing and I would rather people remembered me for the positive side of nature rather than the negative. I was always cheerful and happy and still am to this day and people still comment to this day on my positive and happy outlook on life, I am and always have been one of life's smilers and have been told I have a "cheeky" face which I guess is good, right?

Again, unbeknown to me this was the process I now call "clarity of thought" and the magical "afterbask" at work again, centring my energy and focussing my thoughts and energy and projecting me to "living without" myself as opposed to living "within" myself a concept which we'll explore again later.

So there I was, 22 and single but slowly but surely beginning to earn quite a lot of money and being incredibly happy with it and having a ball as I had only just moved to London from the north of England two years earlier and had gone from what I perceived as a place of familiarity and security to a completely and alien place and I even spoke with a "strange northern accent" which at the time was slightly strange, at least to anyone in London as at that time they were very few northerners living down south.

Again, I came from a place I had grown up in total security, a small town in the north of England, TV, reality TV and social media as we now know it was nowhere near as huge as it is today so the world did indeed seem to be a larger and scarier place!

But it was my inner confidence and my ability to project living my life "without" that brought me so many friends and landed me my first job in a London publishing company.

I've found over the years that if you want to be successful in life, if you're an achiever, if you run your own business, or if you just want positive change in your life, being a wallflower won't do it, that's living your life "within" and by living "within" and this might sound like a contradiction in terms your inner majesty and beauty withers and dies or at the very least doesn't have the opportunity to take root and flourish in the outside world because it never experiences the joy of living in the sunlight, it's never given the opportunity to shine and people only perceive shadow, there's that old saying about "hiding your light beneath a bushel" and that still rings true to this day.

Don't get me wrong, I'm not advocating the life of a "braggadocio" as that will only earn contempt in the long run and living your life from "without" isn't for everyone but again I'm not aiming this book at everyone, it's for those people who want to see real and positive change in their lives, people who want to unleash their true selves, people who want to live in the light, people who want to succeed in whatever shape way or form, and again this will manifest in different ways for everyone for everyone thank goodness is different and individual.

For some success or happiness may equate to weight loss, an increase in self-esteem of confidence, increased fitness or stamina, having material goods or fantastic health for others success in business and monetary wealth and to others it's find that eternal fountain of youth and being able to drink from it again!

What I'm saying is that all this achievable to anyone and everyone by finding your true self, your happy self, your unique and individual self and it's available to everyone by seeking and finding your "clarity of thought", your own personal route to the "afterbask", because within your "afterbask" your true self lives your life "without" and becomes a shining beacon!

CHAPTER 4: One becomes a Pair

Then what happens!

I'm rolling around having a great time enjoying London and all it has to offer when WHAMMO!

I meet a girl!

I'm 22 and she's sweet 16, the most beautiful girl I've ever seen in my life with a flower tucked just so in her hair and I fall head over in heels in love although I have to say in all fairness the feelings weren't immediately reciprocated, much to my chagrin!

But guess what, I smiled a lot and eventually won through and she agreed to go on a date with me and it was one of the most magical and enchanting times I can ever remember having, to this day she was the love of my life and still has and always will have a very special place in my heart.

Within a year we were engaged, she was 17 I was still 22, a year later at 18 and 23 respectively we were married.

Life was so good I can't even begin to tell you, I was so filled with joy it was unreal and my inner self radiated, I lived in a HUGE "afterbask" and everything I ever wanted to be or have simply seemed to fall into place and I was truly living my life from "without" and I had this very special person to share it all with which made it so much more special, so much more joyful!

We bought our first house or should I say a plot of mud which signified our plot and visited every single weekend to see it going up anther couple of rows of bricks, we lived in the countryside at the time and I used to commute to London daily as she did but we used to drive up together which was always a great time and if we couldn't drive home together in the evening she'd get the train home and I would arrive later.

The weekends were always special and we would wander up our local country lane to an eccentric old lady who ran a farm and kept chickens and ducks so we would always have a walk up a local hillside or explore the lanes around where we lived and on the way back stop off and buy some fresh eggs and stop off in the village to buy some bacon and sausages and have a hearty breakfast!

Life was good and the "afterbask" was truly glorious, the sun to my mind at least was constantly shining!

Things just seemed to get better and better, I was really and truly in my element and I was living my life from "without" and because I was coming from a place of true happiness and joy with no feelings of fear and anxiety everything just seemed to flow.

Just having her in my life, sharing my life, doing things together, taking enjoyment in life together was a very happy and powerful place to be.

I don't know if you remember an old TV series from the 60s called the "Persuaders" which starred Tony Curtis who drove a Ferrari Dino and Roger Moore who drove an Aston Martin. As a child, it was one of favourite programmes and my parents would always let me stay up and watch it and I was enthralled by Tony Curtis's character and in particular the car he drove so I'm guessing it was embedded in my unconscious from an early age.

We lived in Kent for about two years and then made the decision to move closer to London for as much as we loved where we lived the daily commute and the long hours were proving to be quite tiring and it made so much more sense to live in a London suburb and only be a short hop into town.

We seemed to search high and low forever and then we struck lucky, even as we walked down the little pathway my wife and

I both knew that this was going to be our new home, it was instinctive and mutual and even though it needed a lot of work doing to it we were up for the challenge. We were in love and young and nothing seemed insurmountable, life was still good and I was still incredibly busy and having a ball because I just so enjoyed what I was doing it didn't seem like work and we had a lovely lifestyle to go with it, nothing pretentious but just a really nice lifestyle and some wonderful holidays abroad and weekends away.

I can't remember who said it but the old adage about finding something that you enjoy doing and you'll never work again was very appropriate for me at the time.

CHAPTER 5: The Afterbask delivers

I was now 25 and my wife was 20 and we were both so incredibly young and in love and full of the joys of life and yet felt so mature (is that feeling recognisable to you).

Now this was when a wonderful thing happened to me, and as luck would have it, or was it the power of the "afterbask" I now ask myself which I was constantly living in remember even though I didn't know it at the time.

Suddenly I realised I had the opportunity to buy myself a Ferrari Dino!

My boyhood car was there and for sale and I had the money and the opportunity to buy it, how awesome was that, how exciting, every boys dream there to be had!

But do you know what, I didn't buy it, for some reason the fit didn't feel right but something had been stirred within me and the hunt was on!

I trawled the newspapers and magazines for days, this was before the days of the internet and finally found and fell in love with an electric blue Ferrari 308 GTSi with tan leather seats, it was the most beautiful machine I had ever seen and I bought it there and then on the spot, it simply called out to me, and the fun and pleasure that car brought to me was indescribable, I was like a child with a brand new toy, I used to love to start it up just to hear the engine noise the snarl of the exhaust and to simply watch the needles dance!

We used to have many weekends away in the English countryside in that car and to this day even as I write these words I feel a thrill of excitement as I think back to it! Vroom! Vroom!

Our home was coming along beautifully as well now, it was hard work but the thrill and excitement of creating our home together brought my wife and even closer than I thought possible and I felt so much love for this girl I can't even begin to describe it to you, she was my joy and I loved her so much and she brought so much pleasure and unbridled happiness into my life.

I used to love surprising her with small gifts like flowers or chocolates and it always gave me such a thrill to watch her face opening gifts or when I had booked a surprise weekend away for us both which always thrilled her.

I've never met anyone as hardworking as her to this day and as well as having a full-time job she worked so hard on that house and was with me every step of the way in whatever we did, painting, stripping wood, building things, you name it, she was the rock in life, my life partner, my soul mate!

It was now 1981 and I had traded up my electric blue Ferrari 308GTSi for a shiny red 308 GTS carburettor model the baby to have and I was still riding my motorbike around London but this time I had moved from the publishing world and entered the realm of the London corporate world which was much more lucrative.

CHAPTER 6: Code of Honour

As I said life and my energy just seemed to flow and all this was so much fun, I very rarely felt tired and had an almost inhuman exuberance and energy, the "afterbask" was so strong in me and it was attracting all the right things into my life and into my universe, I was being true to myself and caring towards others, and honesty and integrity have always been and will always be a code of honour I will always follow and never diminish from.

I will always be respectful to others and never talk down to anyone.

Treat others as you would want to be treated yourself a simple and effective code that works and doesn't cost a thing!

CHAPTER 7: The Beginning of the End

So, 1982 came around and I was working freelance at start up at a small corporate in central London and it was there that my destiny was to take a most unexpected turn although I didn't know it at the time. It was here I was going to experience the biggest highs and lows of my entire life and career thus far, I was going to meet some great people who were going to become great friends and I was also going to meet some not so nice people, this 18 year episode would change the entire course of my life and my life itself, it would be the catalyst that ended my life as I knew and loved but would also serve to teach me some very hard lessons and set my foot along a new path a new life, a path where I would have to go deep "within" myself to discover and feel the joy and the power of the "afterbask" again and to indeed find my true self, my "part two" as I call it now.

I met my future business partner here a seemingly very nice man at the time but I will simply call "The insecure man" a man who would prove to be one of the most insincere and insecure people I ever had the misfortune to meet.

Like all first relationships it all went swimmingly well and bear in mind I was still working freelance graphic designer as was he but he had been put into the company a few weeks ahead of me by the same company who had placed me there and organised freelance artists for corporate organisations so he knew the ropes as it were and it was his responsibility to show me around for the first couple of weeks.

All was good and it was at this place that I began to earn even more money with the added benefit of not having to travel around which seemed very nice at the time and much more convenient.

Within a short period of time the company had approached us and told us that they were terminating their contract with our supply agency but would be very happy if we both decided to stay. It seemed a great idea at the time for as well as working here I was also still able to work at other agencies as well, the perfect solution, for me at least.

The company started to grow quite quickly and got busier and busier which in turn meant I had less time to work at other agencies and had to spend more and more time here as it was becoming my main source of income which was great at the time but as we all know with hindsight and experience it's never a good idea to put all your eggs in one basket.

Life was still good and so was my home life and we were still enjoying the fruits of our labours and still very much in love with each other and life, we had each other, food, a home and wonderful pets, cats, rabbits, canaries and believe it or not a flipping pet rat which my wife adored!

Then one day myself and "The insecure man" were called into a company meeting with one of their directors who was responsible for distributing our workload within the organisation who I'll kindly call "Mr. Shrewd".

He broached the subject of "us" working for them, still on a freelance basis but as partners. The idea seemed to be sound and it was my first taste of what was to become corporate life and my first taste of being "in business" rather than "being a business", scary but exciting at the same time and at this moment in time I had no idea of the true colours of "The insecure man" and his deep insecurities.

So, the company grew as did our partnership and I really felt that was to be "my vehicle" that would bring me even greater success and the material wealth, possessions and lifestyle I sought at that time.

CHAPTER 8: Personal Power

As time went on it became apparent that I was the "organisational brain-the people person" behind the partnership and in effect was running the internal studio and managing the staff therein as "The insecure man" was too involved in the process and didn't have the aptitude for managing people or invoicing etc. so that role naturally fell to me.

Our internal studio continued to grow and "The insecure man" was then positioned in the main building of the company and I set up and ran the "internal studio" from a building across the road a situation which was incredibly effective as it meant we worked as a standalone company and the people management skills, strategies and techniques I learned were absolutely priceless, on the job training that could never be bought and couldn't be taught at this level, you either had to sink or swim and I proved to be a very capable swimmer.

I also had quite a few friends within the company at this time who also shared my passion for motorbikes and we were all crazy mad bikers!

In fact, another route to the "afterbask" for me is riding my motorbike, the thrill, the speed, the sound of the exhaust, the power, the feeling of speed, the exhilaration, the feeling of freedom was awesome and never failed to give me a buzz and still does to this day!

I started off on "Harleys" like most men do but quickly learned to love the Japanese speed bike or "rice rockets" as we affectionately called them and I was a total "poseur" I loved the leathers, the mean look, the way people were slightly wary of bikers just added to it. The biking fraternity is a very special and close brotherhood and often misunderstood and you'd have to be a biker to understand that, it can't be conveyed in words, it's an experience, an emotion almost.

As the years went by the bike gang grew and our yearly trips to France grew and began to get more and more adventurous. In fact, on one particular trip I was so caught up in the "afterbask" the feeling of speed, the thrill of it all that it almost cost me my life!

It was one of the most sobering experiences of my life and I wouldn't ever want to repeat it.

I lost control on a bend doing approximately seventy miles an hour in baking hot heat. I drifted too far to the opposite side of the road and rode head on into an oncoming vehicle!

I was lucky, very lucky, I hit the ground instead of going up in the air and I still maintain that was what saved my life, if I had gone up in the air with my motorbike I would have come down in a crescendo of tangled and burning metal but by hitting the ground I rolled and rolled and ended up laying on my back in the middle of the road. I managed to stagger over to the grass verge and as I took off my crash helmet the only damage to myself was torn jeans a cracked crash helmet and a massive blow to my ego!

I had looked death in the face and survived but I wasn't about to jump about rejoicing, as my mates all converged on the spot with looks of utter shock and horror on their faces the enormity of what had happened washed over me and I quite simply saw a picture of my wife and two little children's faces in my mind's eye and broke down and cried unashamedly in front of everyone, all I wanted at that moment in time was to be in the bosom of my family, the people I loved most in the world and they were a continent away.

I wasn't to be the only victim on that fateful trip, a trip that has gone down infamously in our motor biking lore of the time!

We lost another couple of bikes in impressive smash ups, but what the hell, we were men, it was the eighties, life was good and what a hell of tale to tell everyone once we got back home.

When I got back home and went to pick up my new motorbike a few weeks later the shock of the smash had faded but was brought back to vivid existence as my crashed bike had been picked up and shipped back home for insurance purposes, my brand new gleaming red Fireblade was all polished up and waiting by the kerbside.

I approached confidently keys in hand, but when I saw the mangled tortured, burned out, twisted piece of black metal that had been my previous machine, a cold sweat broke over me and I felt fear!

I knew there and then that if I didn't get on my new bike and ride it I'd never get on another bike again as long as I lived!

I started to have doubts and started to try and negotiate my money back and the shop keeper obviously wasn't very happy. Then a strange thing happened, I went outside, put on my crash helmet and felt a feeling of "awesomeness" coming over me, I had "clarity of thought" and a voice inside my head that was laughing and saying get on that bloody bike and ride it man are you going to let one accident ruin something that brings you so much pleasure, that gains you an additional entry to the "afterbask" no I said in return, jumped on the bike and did what is called a "wheelie" in motorbike terms down the road, it was brash it was kind of stupid but it had to be done.

Wahay! I was back and it was an important lesson I learned in facing my fear and going through it.

My role within the company continued to grow and I was responsible for briefs from not only creatives but also account directors and the traffic department as it was then called and I was in my element as I loved the business aspect of all this, taking the briefs, converting to finished artwork, charging, invoicing being a manager and looking after people which felt like a completely natural role for me.

However, when I start to reflect and look back at this time, although it gave me many life experiences and many business skills I was beginning to have gnawing doubts, niggling little voices inside me that I was ignoring, for at that time I didn't really understand what my "unconscious" was trying to tell me.

"The insecure man" insecurities were beginning to show and manifest, not only in the fact that he never went home and I would constantly have his wife ringing me up on the telephone complaining to me that she never saw him and neither did their kids and even though there was no physical need for him to be there the personal insecurities he felt manifested in the fact that he felt the need to always be there to always seen to be seen which was beginning to cause friction between us.

CHAPTER 9: The Writing on the Wall

It was also the fact that the company had realised how much money we were now making and wanted a much larger slice of our "pie" which I was very happy to do but I wanted it on our terms as well as theirs it had to be fair, it had to be win, win for both sides.

I had numerous lengthy discussions with "The insecure man" and we always came to an agreement on our strategy with upcoming or impeding meetings regarding our future and yet no matter what we agreed between us in every meeting without fail "Mr. Shrewd" would look pointedly at "The insecure man" and ask him "what do you think about this" and every time without fail he would always back down and I would sit there completely gob smacked as to his actions, which were in the fact the actions of a spineless man, a man without any backbone the weakest link in our business chain and "Mr. Shrewd" played this to his advantage mercilessly and to put in bluntly over a very short period of time we "were screwed" the writing was on the wall but I hadn't seen it yet and that was to prove my downfall.

By now I wasn't really enjoying my work life anymore but thank goodness for my daily kickboxing and weight training sessions.

I was now beginning to find these sessions were the best way to release my increasing frustrations with not only the way our partnership was going, which was nowhere but more worryingly the increasing control "Mr. Shrewd" now had over us.

It seems now that I wasn't naturally living in the "afterbask" anymore, I was beginning to live my life from "within" and not "without" and looking back I can feel the empty space that was beginning to grow within me, looking back I can actually "feel" that space as it grew because I'm now more aware but at the time I still naively believed we could turn it around, I still had my honour code and mistakenly believed that would be enough to prevail, constantly do the right thing and surely they would begin to see things from our point of view?

This was incorrect thinking as I now realise our ship had sailed and although I was still "The Captain" I really wasn't navigating anymore, all I was doing in fact was bailing out water, a pointless exercise and the joy had gone out of it, my inner spark no longer shined brightly with my work, although outwardly I never showed it!

To all intent and purposes I was the consummate professional.

The "afterbask" only seemed to come now from my daily workouts, whether it was kickboxing or weight training and when I came back or when I was home with my wife everything felt good again when in reality I was hiding my inner pain and frustration, although never from her, she was always my rock, my listening ear and the biggest support structure I ever had in my life.

This went on for another couple of years and although I was still doing relatively well financially I wasn't enjoying myself but I had also fallen into the trap of "security" or rather perceived security through regular income and a world I knew well, what a pointless existence, sustenance with no substance!

At this time we had through the intervention of "Mr. Shrewd" taken on a third partner without any thought or consideration as to our opinion and our relationship with this individual "Mr. Greed" was always going to be tenuous and strained, he was never our idea of any kind of person we would want to do business with let alone become "business partners" with but little did I realise the enmity and sheer jealousy that would build up within him over time and also as a separate issue with "The insecure man"

It became apparent that "Mr. Greed" wanted my job and of course there was no way that was going to happen unless I left, and also across the road "The insecure man" was slowly and internally festering a huge grudge against me due mainly of the fact I was running the internal studio and basically

27

running and building the business as we were now responsible for servicing not only the main company but also a below the line company they had taken over and also a point of sale company, a huge responsibility, a situation that I can now see rubbed him up when in fact he was incapable of running a business, great at his job, outstanding in fact but no head for the wheels of business and less still for managing people, he couldn't even manage his own time or his own family life let alone other peoples but what I also didn't realise at the time that "Mr Shrewd" was also fanning the flames of discontent behind the scenes.

I realise now that his plan derived from the old concept of "divide and conquer" and boy was he good at it!

CHAPTER 10: Unknowingly Lost

The "afterbask" seemed so far away and the feelings from my workouts, the calm the energy was serving me well but I wasn't heeding the message my unconscious was telling me at the time, I was outwardly successful, great job, cars, motorbikes, wonderful wife and now two gorgeous children but that's all it now was, a job, there was no more fun in it anymore and the fact that I had now moved house with a larger mortgage and also had two small children weighed heavily on my then still young shoulders, I had let myself become trapped and this was an uncomfortable feeling.

I had many grand plans to leave and do other things and try to discover that "joie de vivre again" to feel the warmth of that natural "afterbask" but a terrible thing had happened to me, I had begun to feel FEAR and my timeframe within this particular section of my life was about to come tumbling down around my ears in the most spectacular fashion imaginable!

CHAPTER 11: Betrayal and unbridled Fear

I remember it all as though it was only yesterday, a telephone call from the Financial Director a real "cold bastard" corporate through and through informing me that he wanted to see me in his office immediately and for some strange reason even though I didn't know what it was about I felt a feeling of complete dread, I recalled a much earlier incident with this "Cold bastard" which didn't involve me at all, when I was sat in an office chatting to a director friend when he walked up to the PA outside the office sat at her desk with an envelope in his, he handed it over to her and said very tersely "could you inform the sender of this letter that the stamp on this letter is from our stationery department which makes it tantamount to theft, would you return it to him and tell him what I just told you" my friend and I sat there speechless and couldn't believe what we had just heard but he was deadly serious, this man would penny pinch the cost of a stamp!

It was made even more ridiculous by the "outrageous business expenses" that this man constantly rubber stamped from the company's main department a fact that wasn't lost on anyone.

So, I entered the room and my heart went icy cold as it is doing even now as I recall this incident, the room was set out as what can only be described as a "kangaroo court" with the "cold bastard" in the middle, to the right was the "very nice" traffic manager who was my personal friend but who had a face of steel, completely unreadable. To his left the company lawyer, I felt the colour drain out of my face and my heart drop into my shoes even though I had no idea what this was about it just didn't feel good!

I was asked to sit down by the "cold bastard" who was the only one who did the speaking and was told that there had been some very serious allegations made against me by my fellow director "Mr. Greed" and I sat there open mouthed and completely incredulous as these ridiculous charges were levelled at me, all of which were completely unwarranted, Inwardly I was screaming but I had to steel myself and sit there and listen.

It transpired that I had made what I thought was a minor transgression with an overpayment to an employee which I had completely forgotten about because it had happened about a year previously, the employee had mentioned it to "Mr. Greed" in general conversation and he had logged it and kept it in mind for future reference, "Mr. Greed" had made his power play and he had made it well.

To be truthful it seemed so minor and ludicrous to me at the time I denied it which was a complete mistake, I wasn't being truthful not only to them to also to myself I had dishonoured myself and my own honour code and I was about to pay a huge and heavy price for that mistake!

Quickly realising the error of keeping the lie intact I owned up to it almost immediately as there was no merit in it and I have always been thoroughly honest and thought that would be the end of it.

I really and truthfully believed I would receive a "rollicking" there and then and that would be the end of it, no way, this "cold bastard" had other plans for me and you could almost see the relish and the ugly sneer on his face as he began to "pass judgement" on me.

I sat there not really hearing, I felt the colour drain out of my world, the feeling out of my legs, I felt physically sick and could feel myself beginning to tremble inwardly, I was listening but not believing and I was thoroughly alone with no support whatsoever.

He informed me in that "cold bastard" voice of his that what I had done was very serious indeed as I had breached their trust, they would have to involve the police and if I was found guilty I would be sent to prison, PRISON, I heard those words ringing out aloud over and over in my ears and in my mind, PRISON, surely that's what happened to criminals not me, not to someone who had been there for eighteen years now, who had served them well and had openly admitted to making a mistake, prison was for criminals and I was being made to feel like the lowest form of life on earth.

I was still reeling from that and trying to plead my case when he hit me with another bombshell, I was to be physically escorted off the premises immediately, make no contact with anyone and pick up my belongings and go home. I was to stay at home until one the company's main directors returned from a business trip to the US in three days' time when a final judgement would be made to my fate and whether or not I would be prosecuted!

Shocked, mortified, rocked, stupefied, to this day I can't think of any words that could describe to you the sheer terror and disbelief I felt in those moments and even now years after the event I feel terrible chills running up and down my body as I recall this it was that major and unexpected an event and so callously delivered by work colleagues by people I knew and trusted and no chance of appeal.

I had been tried, judged and basically hung drawn and quartered!

I had to walk through my own company escorted by my friend the "very nice" traffic manager and not allowed speak to anyone at all not even my own brother who I then employed as a studio manager, I was even escorted to the car park, I was so bewildered!

CHAPTER 12: The End of the Beginning

I can't even tell you how I managed that 10-mile drive home through London traffic, I had to stop on several occasions to control myself as the words PRISON kept ringing through my head, I had two small children, a 5-year-old son and a four-year-old daughter at the time what would they do if Daddy went to prison, my gorgeous wife how would she cope with the mortgage and the children with me in PRISON!

I had to stop and throw up it was so terrible so terrifying!

I calmed myself for a few minutes and managed to call my wife on my mobile telephone and tell her as best as I could what had happened which was very difficult as I was so distraught I was in tears, sobbing fitfully and uncontrollably, she couldn't believe what she was hearing and just told me to drive carefully and to get home as best as I could, even in my state I could sense her anguish and her outrage as she had never ever liked me working in that environment and working with those "walking egos" as she used to call them.

I was feeling so much abject terror at this time I don't know to this day how I ever managed to get home in one piece that day, all I know was that God must have been with me.

The power and the joy of the "aftebask", the feeling of living my life "without" myself the sheer sense of fun and pleasure I always felt in my life and in everything I always did that ran through me naturally like rich vein had gone, there was only now only fear, terror unreasoning panic and total blackness.

Unfortunately, that blackness would remain me for a lot longer than even I could imagine.

I made it home and somehow it wasn't comforting anymore, my wife had arranged for the two little ones to be looked after by a friend and I was basically a gibbering wreck, in floods of uncontrollable and unbidden tears, throwing up, incoherent, panic stricken and it took several hours of my wife just holding me close to bring me back to a semblance of normality and that single act of kindness I will always remember with love and fondness.

I had to go to bed and try and sleep I didn't know what to do, of course my family all came around later that day and my brother had to leave work to just to be with me and offer love and support but of course none of this helped, I was in total meltdown, the words PRISON kept ring though my mind.

The one thing I do remember with any clarity of that night is that my Mum stayed the night to look after the kids (bless her) and it was around about 2am when I found myself in their bedroom looking down into their separate cots and taking it in turns to stroke their tiny heads and sob silently as I wondered what would happen if I went to prison!

The callous bastards made no contact with me whatsoever and I had to wait the full three days before I was summoned to their grandiose presence where cow toed, humble and terrified I tried to remain calm in the presence of the "cold bastard" and this time one of the "names of the door" one of the big men himself.

I was then told again how serious "my crime" was but they had decided not to prosecute, I felt a wave of relief shudder through my body but sat silent as I knew they hadn't finished with me yet!

They then passed their infinite and wise judgement upon me, I would be allowed to stay in their employment but there would be conditions, I would be stripped of my directorship and would just become an employee, in other words I would just become one of the guys I used to manage, I wasn't allowed to talk about the true facts around the incident as they would issue a "cover story" and smooth things over to avoid difficult questions and "Mr. Greed" had now in effect become my boss a fact he relished in!

CHAPTER 13: Surrender to Fear

For some unknown reason to this day, I allowed myself to "fall upon their bounty" but I may as well have fallen upon their sharpened blades for they had done me no favours at all. This was now Thursday and I had till Friday to accept and if I did I was to turn up for work as though nothing had happened and take my place as an employee in a company I had helped to build up and run and face everyone knowing the kind of stories "the rumour mill" would be generating and unable to give the true story from my side as it had been forbidden.

I vividly recall no feeling of relief apart from the fact that the dreaded PRISON word no longer hovered over me like the "sword of Damocles" and as the reality and enormity of they had proposed and what I was expected to do started to seep in I just felt numbness.

That Sunday night before I had to go in was one of the worst nights of my life I can remember, again my children had to be taken to my Mums because as much as I loved them my coping mechanisms had shut down completely and I didn't want them to see Daddy crying as I knew I would as soon as I saw their helpless little faces looking at me with wonderful love that only children can.

It was 3am and I was sat in the corner of my bedroom curled up in ball trying to find some kind of solace by cuddling myself to somehow ease the inner pain and torment I was feeling, trying to come to terms with the fact that in a few short hours I would have to enter the doors of a company I had set up and run and now enter it as an employee and worst still face my nemesis "Mr. Greed" the man who had who done his physical best to destroy me and all for the sake of gaining position and power and just as bad face everyone else that I knew.

My brother drove over to my house at 4.30am to be with me and accompany me on my journey to hell that morning, I had discussed the possibility of not turning up of not going through with it with my wife and she was wholeheartedly behind me as I knew she felt only a cold anger and hatred towards those people who had done this to me and would support me in whatever decision I made, but to be truthful I was incapable of any such decision all I saw was the immediate torment and torture I immediately faced and the fact I had a young family to support.

To mine and Gods everlasting pride I made it to work that morning and walked through those doors and to this day I will NEVER EVER know where that strength came from!

And so that was the beginning of one of the darkest years of my life and "The insecure man" was keeping his head down although he did try to offer me some words of comfort but you could tell he wasn't really interested and I now know he was secretly gleeful.

I stuck at this situation for a full year in the belief that friends in the company had told I was merely being punished, I was being given a "slap on the wrist" and my job role and title would probably be given back to me if I "kept my head down", a lie I barely believed through a full year of torturous pain.

I was truly living my life "within" myself now, wrapped up and enveloped in total fear, I had relinquished control of my life, my personal power and my destiny to others.

I was merely going through the motions of life and had no control and I didn't realise at the time that it wouldn't return until I had rediscovered my true self, until I had smashed through that fear and took control of my life and destiny again for in reality no man has true control over another.

I had been mentally destroyed and this was again with hindsight a bizarre healing process I had to go through, for through all this I firmly believed that with the help of my friends within the company my natural popularity and early successes with this organisation which must surely amount to something and count in my favour that sanity would prevail, I would be "wrapped on the knuckles" having been taught a lesson and everything would be ok, what kind of helpless thinking was that and it was to be a thought process and mind-set I would never allow myself get into again EVER!

CHAPTER 14: Cold Reality

Hardship now began to kick in and day to living was adding to the pressure and one of the reasons I was toughing out was in the mistaken belief I would be reinstated.

The beloved Ferrari had to be sold to cover the cost of my salary cut as reflected by my "lowered status", as did our prized Grandfather clock and various other treasured possessions, times were very hard indeed and mortgage payments were becoming increasingly difficult to find which was obviously impacting on my relationship with my wife although we always ensured our children never suffered.

"Mr. Greed" had been trying to flex his new found muscles and was making power plays left right and centre but he wasn't that popular and was beginning to make waves, "The insecure man" was such a weakling and was still backing down from anyone and everything and in fact the only lesson he learned from this ghastly episode was that being subservient kept him out of trouble but he was now sowing his own harvest because his own inability and unwillingness to manage the company we had built together was coming back to bite him hard in arse in the form of "Mr. Greed".

To stop all this infighting, the company then brought into play who I can only describe as "Barabas" and any biblical aficionados will grasp the meaning and implication of that traitorous name straight away.

He was one of my so-called friends from the company or so I thought and I'll never forget him putting his traitorous arms around my shoulders and telling me that "for what it's worth mate I'm a 100% behind you and no one thinks any the less of you for what's happened, if you just let me in on how you used to run the company, briefings, invoicing, systems etc it will work well in your favour".

And you know what, I bloody well believed him there was no reason not to, don't forget I had been there 18 years now so really believed that everyone had my best interests in mind, naïve, trusting, misplaced honour code you take your pick.

Another mistake of character judgement he had seized an opportunity and was merely currying favour with the powers that be and get his feet firmly under the table, for I found out at a later date that this imbecile was so useless at his job in the main company that he was in fact being lined up for the chop, but as he played golf with a "name on the door" had pulled in a favour over a round of weekend golf and "offered to babysit" the company, realising if he played his cards right he could turn it to his advantage.

I was still managing to keep my sanity by working out every opportunity I could and when I couldn't make the gym some of my company friends my brother and myself had constructed a makeshift gym in the basement car park of the main company over the road and we even did some kickboxing down there as well.

I cannot tell you how powerful these daily workouts became, the frustration and anger I was filled up with slowly began to release and those overwhelming feelings of terror coupled with the shame of being demoted were beginning to slowly return and far from being demoralised I was becoming centred again.

This was good because again one year to the day I was summoned to another meeting and as this was apparently my "yearly performance review" I felt positive and as buoyant as I could as I had kept my head down as instructed and made the power transition as smooth and painless as possible by cooperating at every level and I had also been told over the "grapevine" for the last few months that a lot of my friends had been making their voices heard and weren't happy about the situation and the way I had been treated so naively, I fully expected something positive to come from this meeting.

Present at this particular meeting was "Barabbas" and "The insecure man", I greeted them both with a smile for no matter what I thought of "The insecure man" we had been not only partners but "friends" for 18 years oh and as a gesture of kindness on their part they had decided not to invite "Mr. Greed" to this appraisal, how bloody considerate of them!

I was then informed that I hadn't performed as well as expected over the last year and would be getting another pay cut and was indeed lucky not to have been sacked!

CHAPTER 15: Time to reclaim the Afterbask

Shock hit me again but this time I didn't fold, I sat straight and looked them both in eyes and made my point of all the positive and productive things I had done over the past year, MASSIVE shock number two, this is where "The insecure man" finally showed his true feelings and how I had never noticed "the worm in my bosom" for to call him a viper would be an injustice to snakes, the years of resentment and jealousy which had built up in over the years finally emerged in a disparaging snarl and voice filled with barely disguised contempt as he told me "I deserved everything that had happened to me and to expect nothing less".

These low life worms didn't just want my job the company and everything I had helped to build up they wanted to bury me!

You know what happened then... I stood up and laughed out loud, told them exactly what I thought of them without leaving much to the imagination and promptly left the room.

As you can imagine consternation followed for days afterwards and for the first time in a while I felt happy, the daily workouts I had been putting myself through were beginning to serve me well again and I was feeling the benefits of being stronger not only physically but also mentally, I was much more focussed and knew I was not going to take this abhorrent treatment any longer, I had bloody well built up this company not these two idiots who were daring to JUDGE ME on MY performance when the main reason the company had been so successful over the years was because of ME!

Over the next week or so they tried to make things even more unpleasant but how was that possible, they had done their worst to me and I had survived, I hadn't died, I hadn't gone to prison, I had stayed true myself to my own honour code throughout this last year and these were sad little men trying to further their own careers and make themselves feel big at my expense, NO WAY!

I spent a couple of days speaking to a solicitor just to know what kind of position I was actually in and found that the law as it stood at time highlighted the fact that I been there for over 18 years, and I was in effect being "constructively dismissed" and as a consequence I was actually entitled to a nice sum of money for every year that I had been there, which was great news to me, so armed with this information I used this wonderful feeling of being in my power and living my life "without" myself again to gain the spiritual fuel I needed to draft a beautiful professional and constructive letter stating how I felt at the way I had been treated and how I had a case for "early leaving" I arranged another meeting with them and in anticipation of this I put myself through a punishing physical workout comprising of weights and kickboxing, I was pumped, I showered and I felt the "afterbask" fill my entire being and with it came "Clarity of Thought"!.

I presented them with this letter in person and also sent a copy to every bloody main director in the company, I was sick and tired of running in fear I had regained my power and even though I had lost the major battle there was no way I was going to lose any more scuffles with this lot, I'd had enough, I should have seen the writing on the wall previously but initial terror and fear had kept me down and then basically my good and trusting and honest nature had incorrectly believed that the milk of human kindness would show through and justice would prevail, it wouldn't and I'd had enough I was going out with a BANG I was going out standing tall and proud!

CHAPTER 15: Healing process

It was finally over and my honour code had prevailed and I walked out of that place with my head held high but this was just the beginning of yet another adventure in the journey of my life and one that would again test my resolve, my faith in myself, God, the Universe and my ability to feel the afterbask ever again, I was about to be tested to my physical and mental limits!

I felt only relief and the resurgence of my spiritual and mental power but there was no hiding form the fact I had taken a battering and I was very damaged and I still bear the emotional scars of that encounter to this day and it's something I have to work on once in a while and the healing process continues.

We were still struggling financially to be honest and didn't know if we would be even able to keep our house, we had lost so much already that we had worked so hard for but were determined to keep the house at least as this was also home to our two little babes and our main priority was to love, feed, house and clothe them.

I now had a lump sum in the bank, not a huge amount but enough to take the worry and pressure off for about 6 months while I decided on my next move and I knew it had to be a bold one, I had suffered collateral damage in more ways than one but I was born a fighter I was born to float and run free within the afterbask and my daily and now yearly workouts were legendary and I had not only become fitter and stronger I had forged an iron will of steel and there were new horizons to be conquered and experienced and enjoyed.

I spent six months working in my garden and spending time with my little ones taking them to school, to the park and trying to rekindle the old flames of fun and romance into mine and my wife's relationship, I loved all three of them so much with so much passion they were a an integral part of my very being, my life blood the centre of my universe and one of my main reasons for living and going through what I had the previous year, I so wanted to give my lovely wife everything back that we had lost not only materially but also emotionally and spiritually.

She had been such a rock for me, such a support that my love for her grew even greater, she had gone through so much, keeping up my spirits, loving me, holding me, caring for me showing me true love and standing by me when the times were really hard I wanted her to really enjoy life again, I wanted us both to have fun again!

I also must credit to some wonderful people who never lost faith in me and always treated me with kindness and respect the kind of loyalty and emotions those people who had tried so hard to hurt me would never ever experience in their lives as they had no capacity beyond self.

I was in my power again, I was in the bosom of my family my true afterbask and I enjoyed every precious second of time I could spend with them.

Chapter 16: Out of the darkness?

So, I was feeling reenergized, the old me was almost back and I had learned to laugh again and I was feeling the need to get busy again, after all I had spent my entire life being busy and happy and "living without" and that old me was bursting to get out again, to start a new adventure to put the past behind me and move forward like I always have done and still to do this day advocate it as a course of action to others.

It's great to revisit the past and learn from your mistakes but if you're constantly going back there you've never actually moved on, have you?

Learn the lessons and vorwarts mein freund!

Now I had always liked the idea about setting up and running my own design studio, being independent and being answerable to no one but myself and to a certain extent I had followed that pathway but I detoured in the 80s and that was a mistake I wasn't about to repeat.

I was now doing a little freelance work here and there as an apple mac operator and again I was starting to feel confident again and was making relatively good money although nowhere near where I actually wanted to be and felt the need gnawing and growing inside me to move on, feel "The Afterbask" get in my power and do it!

I could feel the glow of "The Afterbask" within me again and it was like being reunited with a long-lost friend and magic things were beginning to happen again, I could feel it, sense it, it was palpable. My workouts were going fantastically well, and I was incredibly happy either "hitting the weights" punching a bag or having a sparring session, "the force" was indeed strong in this one again!

I was feeling happier and if it's the right word for me fairly "contented" but I always like to live on the edge and love being involved in exciting projects, different things to get your teeth into to but always with an end in mind and always serving a higher purpose.

My two gorgeous little kids had their Daddy back in mind as well as body and things had seemingly settled down with my wife but little was I to know the seeds that were being sown there, the crop that was just under the surface waiting to spill out.

It was at this point whilst working in a tiny little company that a friend of mine was running in Soho that I met whom I can only refer to without any malice as "The Weasel" who was then that company's financial director and as this story unfolds you'll begin to understand why I chose that particular name for him.

We started to chat over cups of coffee and once he found out I had worked at "The Company" for such a long period of time he was immediately impressed as at this time this was one of London's premier companies and to have worked there for as long as I had held great sway within that company and I was also a respected name within the industry.

I've always trusted unconditionally, rightly or wrongly until proved otherwise and I wasn't about to let my "Annus Horriblis" ruin me as a basic person so I accepted him at face value and between us we started to formulate the plan to put together a multimedia agency in central London and using my contacts and know how network through "corporate land" and pick up their overflow work and take the headache away from them. I would run the company as MD and he would be my partner as my FD but still keep his full time within this small company and we would meet every day as he was only around the corner and have "brainstorming" sessions" and weekly and monthly financial meetings to discuss cash flow etc. and work out strategy etc. so together we started a company and began a search for suitable office space.

Chapter 17: Luck be a lady

"The Afterbask" was with me and my thinking hadn't been as clear as this for a while, clarity of thought was an everyday occurrence as I now had a sense of purpose, a mission and I was feeling empowered again!

After looking at several office spaces all of which didn't have the "right vibe" we found a beautiful building right in the middle of London's Carnaby Street, how awesome was that and the rent was just right and fell right into our budget and business plan. We had both put in £10,000 each as working capital as we didn't feel the need to apply for overdraft facilities, which was to prove to be a mistake and with hindsight which is an awesome gift wouldn't you agree we might have made a different decision and the outcome could have been so very different but then I wouldn't be following the path "The Afterbask" and the universe truly had in mind for me, it was just going to let me come to that conclusion in the most mind blowingly awesome method it could possibly come up with, the biggest kick in the pants man had ever received!

So, we moved in and gave ourselves a start-up date three months from hence but we had a lot of work to do to make this place into a company and we still had to source our staff which of course as MD fell to me which wasn't a problem as I had a huge base of contacts. I brought my younger bro in as my studio manager as we had both been very close since an early age and as he could no longer work at "The Company" he also wanted in.

Chapter 18: Brotherly love

I feel I should mention at this point the incredible bond and closeness I shared with my brother, even though he was six years younger than me I had always looked after him, I always made sure he had extra spending money but instead of just giving it to him willy nilly which would have been wrong as there wouldn't have been any value to it, he earned it by doing various tasks, nothing arduous or unpleasant but just enough to feel that he actually earned it.

When I got married and he was now an adult we still spent time together, in fact we spent so much time together sometimes that my wife would complain that he seemed to be living with us but I love my family and I loved my younger brother and never tired of spending time with him.

He used to help me with any gardening or chores when he came around and would ask my opinion of things and we would chat for hours and discuss my comic collection of marvel Superhero's and who our favourite character was.

We both loved science fiction and he was into martial arts while I was into weight training, I introduced him to the joys of weight training and the "The Afterbask" and he in turn introduced me to martial arts, to my mind the marrying of the two was absolute perfection, the ying meeting the yang "The Afterbasks" perfect mate and together there could only come magic, they complemented each other beautifully, the martial arts brought a whole new dimension to my life, fluidity, the use of power, foot movements, balance, coordination, strategy, discipline and coupled with my weight training which also used these self-same principles but in very different ways, this was to be my proving ground for the rest of entire life but it also formed and strengthened the bond of our brotherhood.

When he got, older and started driving I went with him when he bought his first car, a beautiful MGB Roadster and most weekends I would get the Ferrari out and he his car and together with our buddies go and burn some rubber around the country lanes and if there was a motorbike shop along the way, preferably a Harley Davidson dealership so much the better as that was the weapon of my choice in those days we were ecstatic, young men living in "The Afterbask".

He used to have games nights around his house and invite me round and it would be great to have a "lad's night out" and generally take the mickey out of each other.

I really loved my brother and he had also stood by and supported me fully when I been demoted and on those days when he could see me suffering he would come over and give me one of his pep talks, bless him, he used to bolster me up my using fighting and kickboxing analogies as he knew I would respond to that, he was wise beyond his years we used to joke that he was my "older younger brother" and I loved him for it!

When my son was born, it seemed logical to me that he would be Godfather and my wife agreed as she had grown quite fond of him at the time and again when my daughter was born thirteen months later the honour fell to little bro again, he was so much more to me than a brother and I rejoiced in his company.

Chapter 19: Launch

I had also had a very close friendship with "The Fox" who had been the handyman at "The Company" and he proved absolutely invaluable in helping us get the office up and running, putting up work benches, building cupboards etc, a true friend and again someone I hold in the highest regard as he was one of the chosen few who also helped me through those dark days at "The Company" with his moral support.

We wanted the office to be functional yet we wanted it to have a "comfort" feel about it at the same time and this was where my wife came into her own, she turned out to be the "mistress of fabrics" and did wonderful things with the décor in our office right down to helping me choose the right furniture and picking the colours and my brother was sourcing our computers and systems, we were an awesome team and at this time "The Weasel" was still a apart of it although he was never around when there was any real graft to be done, I guess he thought his cheap unflattering suits would get even more misshaped.

I had also been incredibly busy and had interviewed loads of people and I had made the conscious decision to only have young student type people around, for one the salaries would be lower but to be honest this wasn't my primary concern as I was more interested in their enthusiasm and work ethic and wanted people I could "steep" in my culture and people who were hungry to learn and wanted to feel part of something very exciting as well.

So, there we were, the "hit team", myself who was going to be responsible for new business, bro as studio manager and two youngsters ready to go!

I had been busy over the weeks and hadn't been idle on the new business front and I had ruthlessly pushed my credentials as an ex from "The Company" person and this in itself opened doors that wouldn't have been available to everyone, it was my "platinum card" the key to the door and I was canny enough to capitalise on it and had managed to secure some business to get us up and running, we were off!

"The Afterbask" had seemingly returned for good!

The weeks and months simply flew by and as they did certain problems began to materialise, "The Weasel" never turned up for meetings, missed coffee morning chats and a tad more worrying at the time but not a major concern not turning up for our allocated weekly and monthly financial meetings which meant I never really knew where we were financially although he assured me the figures were ok and as he was my financial director I didn't really have any reason to doubt him, for anyways, I was so busy on the telephones and going out there getting the work and at this time we were also moving into multimedia for at that time it was still relatively new and I could see the huge potential in that market.

We decided to take on a new employee who specialised in multimedia at the time and before long I had a few contracts because of this and the client list I had was pretty impressive and I was getting work at some stage or other from every major London advertising agency and also the not so large ones, my reputation was growing and the trust and relationships I had built I up over the years was proving to be a godsend, people liked me and if people like you they'll do business with you and when you're in "The Afterbask" working from "without" happiness and trust radiate outwards and people pick up on it, people still comment to this day on how positive and happy I am because to be honest, I am!

I love people, I love life and I have this inner energy and fantastic enthusiasm that shines outwards and I've always, even before I knew how to, tried to be a positive influence on others.

Chapter: 20 Warning bells

Outwardly things were going fine but inwardly I was beginning to feel an unease, my clarity of thought wasn't firing like it should have been for I was constantly chasing up "The Weasel", whether it was for meetings or even for something as simple as petty cash he simply wouldn't turn up when he promised and the amount of hours I wasted not only myself but also by sending my staff around to his office to pick up cash for goods or even just supplies like tea and coffee was frustrating to say the least. He would say to come around for a certain time to meet him and you'd turn up and he'd be in a meeting and keep you waiting in reception until he finished, not only was this rude it was totally unprofessional and a complete waste of time, I felt totally helpless as I could now see the folly of my agreeing to him having control over the company finances, in my rush to get back on track after the dark days I hadn't spent enough time in "The Weasels" company and if I had realised then what a slimy, slippery, insidious little power playing creep he really was I never would have got into business with him, but now it was too late and I had to try and make the best of it.

This went on for months and months and at one point we were desperate for some ink cartridges for our large format printer as I had secured a huge order and they wanted a load of prints by a certain time. I had sent several messengers around to him at the "appointed hour" to pick up the cash and every time they had come back to say, "The Weasel" was in a meeting and he hadn't even the courtesy to leave the money with the receptionist. You have to understand that at this time we were trying to buy things for cash for greater discounts and because he never even allowed us a petty cash box I had to literally beg for every penny off him for everything.

I had called him at 9am to ask him for this cash as I knew we had to get the materials to get the job done on time.
I came to the end of my patience when despite several urgent telephone calls on my part and several visits by my staff it had now got to 6pm!
I was furious to say the least and decided I was going to go around to his office and regardless of if he was in a meeting or not barge in and get that cash off him by hook or by crook, how dare that slimy, big eared little jumped up fart think he could treat us all like this, treat me like this, his bloody partner, I was furious, especially when there was such a huge job on and it now meant the boys would have to work through the night to get it finished and delivered.

49

I went around to the office only to be told "The Weasel" had gone to the pub for a drink with the boss of the small company he worked for, I asked which pub it was and luckily it was a pub in Soho I knew well and as I rounded the corner there he was the miserable little snit laughing and joking with his boss as though he didn't have a care in the world totally oblivious to the fact to the consternation and trouble he had caused my his actions.

I marched straight up to him said hello politely to his boss who I knew personally and asked, "The Weasel" to come around the corner with me so I could speak to him in private. I was totally disgusted with him, as he turned to smile at me I could smell the beer on his breath and it was clear by his eyes that while he had been giving me the run around he had been here drinking for some time.

He was supposed to have £150 on him for materials, money I had asked him for since 9am that morning and now it was almost 7pm, I had spent the entire day chasing this little fop. He tried to put his arm around my shoulder to apologise and pulled £50 out of his pocket saying that was all he had had time to get out, I was so filled with rage at this time which is so incredibly rare for me it surprised me. I remember I had to stand there for several minutes to calm myself before I throttled the life out of him as he not only our own staffs time he had jeopardised an important contract.

With barely controlled rage I pushed him hard against a wall with my hand around his throat and felt a deep loathing for "The Weasel" a feeling I hadn't felt for a long long time, in that split-second I wanted to push his face in but managed to hold back as he started begging me not to hit him, he was pathetic, a scurrilous, despicable apology for a man.

I forcibly composed myself and asked him to accompany me to the cash machine to get out the rest of the money, which the snivelling little wretch did.

I went back to the office and luckily, we managed to finish the job but there was no joy in it for me and I knew I had to find a way to rid myself of "The Weasel" he had violated my honour code but worse still I felt I had violated my own honour code by losing my temper and I wasn't feeling proud of myself!

Chapter: 21 Lost again

I was feeling so low, clarity of thought had left me again left me and I really had no idea how I was going to rid myself of "The Weasel" as he was my partner and I visited several lawyers only to be told the same thing, it would be very difficult.

My great dream of greatness was now floundering quite badly because again I had given away my power and shared it with "The Weasel" and now I was paying the price, there was nothing else I could, I had to try and make the best of a bad job. Chin out, chest high, be stoic and make it work.

I wasn't feeling "The Afterbask" as a powerful tool anymore, my workouts did still give me pleasure but now more as a release for the increasing frustration I was now feeling being tied to someone I had no regard for and also had no respect for really hit a raw nerve for me, I felt trapped, helpless and as you know from what I've previously written these feelings don't sit well with me, I have to feel the joy, feel the sun on my face, the rain beating down, the breath of the wind and all I felt was cold and darkness. The universe was trying to tell me something and I just wasn't listening.

I now know that 55% of any communication is physical and you give out these signals unconsciously and people pick them up and read them all the time, 38% of any communication is verbal and at that time my feelings were so low I had lost my access to "The Afterbask" again and worse I was coming from "within" again and I was clearly giving out these signals.

My relationship with "The Weasel" was going from bad to worse and as a consequence business was beginning to suffer, don't forget I was that business and if I wasn't operating to full capacity neither would the business although I didn't realise it at the time, I just kept hoping things would work out and as we all know or should know, hope is just an intangible road to nowhere.

I tried to make the best of it and gave out office space to creative director and his team who had lost their office but still had some good accounts but again this was to prove to myself once and for all that once I lose clarity of thought, once I come from "within", once I can't access "The Afterbask" I'm in serious trouble.

Chapter 22: "Your worst nightmare" arrives

So, I took on a creative director "Your worst nightmare" who unknown to me had a serious drug problem and marched to the beat of "uncle Charlie" and was completely volatile because of this.

"Your worst nightmare" was unpredictable and prone to mood changes and had to be handled carefully but with him he brought accounts and some much needed cash flow in the form of rent!

Our earlier decision to not arrange overdraft facilities were beginning to take their toll and I really regretted being influenced by "The Weasel" as he assured me in his capacity as financial director that we didn't and wouldn't need it, and those words were ringing in my ears. It wasn't that we weren't busy but many big agencies were taking us to 60 days on our invoices and some of the even larger ones to their eternal disgrace weren't paying us for 90 or even 120 days!

This was having a terrible toll but the exact price we were paying wouldn't become apparent to me for a short while yet.

We employed a "factoring" company to takeover our invoices which seemed like a good idea but it really wasn't as we were paying a fair percentage back to them for taking on the debt and the pressure was building and little did I realise how dramatically it was going to explode or even the catastrophic meltdown it would cause and like any meltdown the effects would be felt for many years to come and many innocent people would fall victim.

I was low; I started to dread going into my own building for it now signified everything I didn't want in life anymore. I hadn't taken a salary for months and relied on the "drip feed" of cash "The Weasel" allowed me when a factoring debt came in and it was miserable. The man I truly despised was controlling my finances and I was dependant on his largesse as I had no access to company funds whatsoever.

I'd taken legal advice a couple of times and tried to get "The Weasel" off my back but was told it would be much too difficult as we were 50/50 partners and it would be very costly indeed and bear in mind I had lost complete clarity of thought and was no longer experiencing the joy and glory that was "The Afterbask" and because of this I was primarily "living within", surviving, basically plodding through life, putting one foot in front of the other and really feeling the pressure again for the second time in my life and it was horrid!

I couldn't pay my mortgage, I couldn't buy things for my children and it was very difficult to even arrange family days out as we were struggling to pay our bills and also put food on the table. I used to pray to God to give me strength to find a way out of this, to show me the way, to light my path to give me a sign, to tell me what to do next...please!

I hated to see my lovely wife having to make do, It hurt me deep inside not being able to provide, I was beginning to feel not only helpless but worthless as I felt I was letting my wife and children down.

I loved them all so much and had so many grand plans and dreams for them and I could now see them fading and disappearing and in front of me was a world of pain and all of a sudden that pain would become very real!

"The Weasel" went away for six weeks' honeymoon and in the first few days chaos began to reign. The telephones never stopped ringing with people ringing up asking when they could expect their cheques and even worse a lot of these people were personal friends, people who had helped me set up because they believed in me and my project, people who had gone out of their way to help me.

I was confused and bemused for many of the people who called I recalled actually signing their cheques when "The Weasel" had sent them over or made a rare appearance for me to counter sign so I had no idea what was going on but deep inside me something felt terribly wrong!

This went on for another two weeks and then I decided to take some advice as "The Weasel" was also incommunicado, and brought in a friend of mine who specialised in "insolvency" and asked him to investigate.

This would take about two weeks I was informed and all I could do was fend off the telephone calls the best I could, get in some more business and try to move forward through or wait until "The Weasel" came back from his honeymoon and sort it out that way but I had no idea at time to the extent of this malingering wretch's machinations.

All I could do was wait, yet inside me a darkness grew, a feeling of dread so powerful it was almost overwhelming it was like the portent of doom, the harbinger of everything dreadful seemed to permeate the atmosphere and I felt yet again, lost, lonely and the gnawing of fear, something was wrong, very wrong!

Chapter 23: The Black Hole deepens

I went home that night and later on that evening I had a telephone from my brother in law which was very strange for he was not the type of bloke to call for even though we were related we never called each other.

The news was very grave indeed, my father in law who I was pretty close to and incredibly fond of had died suddenly and he was calling me because obviously, my sister in law was much too distraught to speak, in fact I could hear her sobbing loudly in the background. I thanked him quietly and then steeled myself for what I had to do, how on earth do you tell your wife that her beloved father has died, how do you do it so there is no shock, no pain, no hurt, it's impossible, no matter how gently you break the news and to make matters even worse it was her last surviving parent as her Mum had died while my wife was in her twenties so she had grown very close to her Dad especially in recent years and in light of the fact he had moved hundreds of miles north with his new wife as her Dad had separated and divorced her Mum many years previously.

I was also very close to him and very fond of him as we had many trips up north to visit him and he always made me very welcome and many an evening after dinner we would sit sipping brandy until the wee small hours and I would listen in amusement as he put the world to rights. But we also had so much in common, we both loved bodybuilding, we loved working out and he had worked out most of his life so we had an immediate affinity and bond as "fellow trainers" and spent many hours chatting about bodybuilders of a bygone age, sport, drug use in modern training and he would amuse us endlessly by repeating tales that we had heard so many times before about the trainers in his gym when he was a young man and also the tales of his adventures.

This man was a poet, passionate, grounded and great fun to with and he told these tales as though he was telling us for the first time and me and my wife would sit there nodding and grinning and listening even though we had heard it so many times before, so yes, I was very close to this man. Also, he had been a huge part of my wife's life in recent years so in turn mine and I felt this loss deeply!

The onus was on me, deep breath and....

I've never seen grief like it in my entire life, she let out a scream and sobs which came straight from her soul, and it was chilling to hear!

She collapsed to the kitchen floor in complete and utter shock then in a complete frenzy started to beat her fists on the floor and physically start to tear her own hair out. I didn't know what to do or how to react if I'm honest, I felt my own heart go out to her, to see the woman I loved so much in this kind of pain, I wanted to hold her to tell her everything would be all right but I knew it wasn't and it wouldn't be, it couldn't be, her entire world she had built around her father had just been torn down in the cruellest way possible.
I went over and tried to hold her just to stop her from hurting herself and in her blind grief she screamed NO at me at the top of her voice and pushed me so hard I crashed into one of the kitchen cupboards, I tried to approach her once more but she was screaming at me not to touch her and you know what something inside just for a split second told me I had lost this woman forever!

My son and daughter who were only six years and five years respectively came to the top of the stairs crying and asking what was wrong with Mummy and I didn't know what to tell them, I just remember making sure my wife was as ok as she could be and then brought the children down to the lounge and tried to comfort them as best as I possibly could but even they sensed that their little lives were about to change as I could see the fear in their little faces as they tried to fathom out was going on with their Mum.

So, the night wore on and I eventually managed to get the children settled and in bed and an uneasy peace fell over the house as my wife had collapsed in a grief and sob ridden sleep on the settee and all I could do was keep watch over her and comfort her the best I could.

A couple of days later she got the train with her sister and brother and went up north to make the funeral arrangements.

I didn't go into the office for a couple of days as I had to look after the kids and my Mum also came over to help which was absolutely fantastic as they have both always been close to their Granny so they had a bit more stability around as well as Dad and I knew my brother was more than capable of looking after the company and the insolvency man was still going through papers and records so it was a case of looking after the kids until she arrived back and giving them loads of attention.

I should point out that at this stage I wasn't aware of any emotions within myself either, just felt drained and spent, clarity of thought and "The Afterbask" were no longer present and indeed it felt as though they had never even existed, this was a dark place and about to get even darker!

Chapter 24: The Wicked Witch!

A week went by and even though I was speaking to my wife on the telephone daily it was becoming a strain and stressful as she was growing more and more distant with each call and there was nothing I could do about it, I felt so helpless as I so wanted to be with her, yet she had insisted I don't accompany her and to be honest the children needed my stability and presence and I had to be close due to the circumstances of the company.

Then I received a call off her to say that she was coming home that evening but not till very late and could I pick her but her voice was very cold and for some reason I felt a chill.

Her train arrive about 2am and she got in, I remember clearly, I tried to give her a kiss on the cheek and she turned away. The conversation on the 40-minute drive back home was muted and strained and then she announced to me that the funeral arrangements had all been made, the funeral would be the following week and she wanted me and my brother to be there which I thought was strange way to put it for of course I'd be there it was a given I was her husband for heavens sake, anyway I didn't push it.

Then she hit me with a statement that I've never understood to this day, "my sister and her husband and my brother will stay at my Dad's house and I've made arrangements for you to stay at a bed and breakfast"!

At first I couldn't believe my ears as I thought I'd heard it wrong, I had to stay in a bed and breakfast, me, her husband of eighteen years who had known her father for that same amount of time and whom I counted as a dear and close friend in fact I even loved him in my own way and I'm sure he felt the same way and my brother in law who hardly knew him was being allowed to stay at his house. I was totally shocked and upset and it cut through me like a knife, not just because of the words being said but also in the incredibly cold way they were being spoken to me as well.

I bit my lip and stayed silent; this wasn't the time to say anything.

The rest of the drive home was in almost total silence although she did tell me to slow down a couple of times.

When we got home I wanted to surprise and please her because I hadn't told while she away that I redecorated our bedroom and done it in her favourite colours as she was always unhappy with the décor and layout. I had also put a picture of her father on the bedside cabinet and had a lit candle in front of it so she could see that I had been thinking of her.

My Mum was also staying because she was helping me with the kids and she was fast asleep in the spare room.

What happened next will be ingrained in my memory forever and to be honest even now it's very painful to be writing about this but it's finally time to let it go I guess.

As I showed her our bedroom and her father's picture she showed no emotion, she just said "you've worked hard but we need to speak". Well let's wait for the morning I said, you've had a terrible week and long journey have a bath and go to bed and we'll chat in the morning.

"I want to chat now, I've been thinking about this for the last few days and I don't love you anymore and I want a divorce and I want you to leave now"!

I thought I was hearing things but she just kept going on and on about how she'd had enough and she was hoping that my company would be successful before she had to tell me but it was too late and she didn't want me in her life, she was unhappy and had been for years and wanted out.

I tried to reason with her as I just kept thinking keep her calm it's the grief, the loss, the tiredness just let her have a bath and go to bed and sleep and we could talk in the morning and sort it out, but no way, she wasn't having it and started screaming at me how she wanted me out.

This of course woke up my Mum who had loved my wife since she was introduced to the family at sixteen and loved her like a daughter.

My Mum tried to reason with her but she just stood there like an ice-cold statue, cigarette in hand snarling at me with such malice I was taken aback.

My emotions were still raw from the previous year and I was dealing with "The Weasel" and company business and just hadn't the emotional tools to deal with this, my rock, the woman who meant so much to me, the love of my life literally was here spitting venom at me in the coldest most sadistic way possible.

This went on for days and days and I was hoping she would calm down with my Mum being able to hopefully talk some sense into her so I tried to maintain some kind of frameworks and normality to my crumbling life by going to the office, to escape for a short while if nothing else.

Chapter 25: Then yet another bombshell!

We then found out from my insolvency friend that "The Weasel" had not only not paid tax or national insurance contributions for me but also hadn't paid them for all our employees and the insidious little snake had fooled my brother into signing a document telling him it was for company business and nothing important yet was in fact his resignation as a company director, he had also withdrawn his share of the monies somehow out of our company account without letting me know.

The cowardly bastard had gone away on his six-week honeymoon and left us to crash and burn!

I was told I had to close down immediately, that we were trading illegally!

I had to sit down and felt myself trembling and close to tears. I asked him if he had got all his facts absolutely clear and he assured me that he had. I called a company meeting and had to tell all my loyal employees the extent of "The Weasels" treachery.

So I started the winding up process without any support from my wife, all I was getting from her was silence at home but while I was at the office during the day she would only give vitriol, spite and venom as she waged her psychological campaign to get me out of her life and the matrimonial home I just couldn't take it, I loved her so much and we had gone through so much and yet here she was when I needed her support more than anything, hurting me in the most unimaginable way possible, I wouldn't have spoken or treated my worst enemy the way she spat her words at me, and when I went home in the evenings she sat there in total and complete silence in the same room as me watching the same TV programmes, if she wasn't in the same room as me she would be in the garden sitting under the scented pergola I had made especially for her talking to her mother law for hours at a time and completely ignoring me, she even used to cook for herself and the children and leave me to cook for myself, it was so incredibly painful I thought my heart was going to burst with anxiety and sadness, it was the greatest feelings of sadness and loneliness I had ever felt in my life , it was like she had died and yet I wasn't allowed to mourn her, look but don't touch.

The Wicked Witch was winning, I had nothing left, and she was making my life a misery and kept insisting I leave the marital home. How could I, I had two gorgeous little children the absolute centre of my universe there, how could she not see this, why wouldn't she let us try again, why, why, why?

I finally and begrudgingly managed to get her to a marriage guidance counsellor hoping that that there my just be a glimmer of hope that could be found no matter how slim, anything to just be given another chance, anything to make things right between us, I still loved her so very much.

She sat there dressed in black, back ramrod straight, cigarette held high magnificent and gorgeous in her cold beauty and refusing to look at me. She just kept repeating over and over again like a worn out record no matter what the counsellor said, "can you tell this fucking bastard I don't love him anymore and I want him out of my life" over and over, words I will never forget till the day I die!

I was doing my best to hold myself together not only for me, but also my children my brother and my employees but you can't seriously fight and win a war on two fronts when you haven't got the resources and this was too close to the previous year when I had almost lost everything at "The Company".

Chapter 26: Knife thrust!

The funeral day arrived and she had been up there a few days beforehand and I travelled up on the train, when we got to my father in laws house it was packed, with some people I knew and with a few I didn't.

My wife opened the door and I went to give her a welcoming cuddle and she spat back at me with her lips curled back "don't touch me"!

Everyone in the room looked slightly taken aback but I just dealt with it and walked in feeling very uncomfortable. She avoided me at all times, wouldn't look even look at me, even on the day of her father's funeral even though she knew how much I revered her father and how upset I was as well, as this man had been a major part of my life as well.

I really don't know what was happening that day or who was responsible for the arrangements but the cortege arrived and the cars to pick up the immediate family and the mourners everyone set off and my brother and myself found ourselves stood on the lawn having been completely missed, there was no car for us we had to make our own way there. I was so pleased that my brother was there for amidst the chaos, pain and confusion he was keeping me together and I was truly thankful for his presence.

So, we arrived at the chapel and the immediate family went to sit at the front row, I went to join my wife and sit at her side and she told me that wasn't my place they had made arrangements for me and my brother to sit tree rows back!

If a blunt rusty knife had been thrust into my heart it couldn't have hurt anymore, I was broken, devastated, confused and I thank god, my brother was next to me for I have no idea what I would have done otherwise.

My heart broke into so many pieces it has never been whole since!

So, when we arrived back in London I had to make the most painful decision I had ever had to make in my entire life. I had to leave the marital home and everything I had worked, everything and everyone I cherished and loved more than anything in the world, my safe haven, my universe of love.

I had to leave my two little ones, a six-year-old boy and a five-year-old girl who adored their Daddy. I spent that night in their bedroom, stroking their heads and crying and couldn't stop telling them how much I loved them, I felt as though a part of me was actually dying that night and in reality, it was.

It's burned into my memory, the scene as I stood in the hallway, my son stood there with tears in his eyes his arms firmly at his side trying not to cry but his little eyes already filling up and his bottom lip quivering, my gorgeous little daughter hanging on to my legs crying Daddy please don't go, my Mum still trying to plead with my wife to come to her senses before it was too late.

It was not to be, she just stood there ramrod straight yet again with still another cigarette in her hand showing no emotion and simply said "you better go now"!

Chapter 27: End game

"The Weasel" still wasn't through with his insidious little games, he had paid some of his "cronies" off to pretend that they were our biggest creditors and I have very little knowledge of company law and he managed to close us down immediately and put us in the hands of his "preferred liquidators" the most unscrupulous bunch of operators I had ever come across, I had no chance, I wasn't even on this planet if the truth was known, not even this universe, I was beaten a shadow even had more substance than me at the time.

To this day, I still don't understand the extent of "The Weasels" treachery and his underhand machinations; however, I'm sure Karma will prevail at some stage.

I had nothing left and nothing seemingly to gain, I was in so much pain, such abject misery I needed an escape, and I found it in the company of "Your worst nightmare".

This man was dangerous in ways I couldn't even conceive, larger than life, outspoken, liaising with unsavoury characters and strangely compelling to be around at the time and he always had access to cocaine, yippee, my escape route to "happiness" and oblivion!

I fell into a routine of going out to night clubs with this man and his friends, complete strangers. Drinking vodka martini like it was going out of fashion and pushing as much white powder up my nose as I possibly could, I wanted to forget the pain, blanket out the loneliness, to lose myself in a world of carousing.

I was treading a very dangerous path and didn't realise it at the time but my wake-up call was around the corner.

I was now living with my Mum, a grown man living with his Mum, I had lost everything, I had no conceivable income, no family to my mind, no one to love, I was frightened, lost, alone and naked.

Instead of going back to my Mums because I was so ashamed of what I was up to I was spending nights in the office in Carnaby Street, for although the company was closed I still had keys to the building for another month. I was going back either drunk or coked up and most evenings both, I was too far gone to even contemplate riding my motorbike home.

Chapter 28: Wakeup call

My mobile telephone rang at 7am, I'd had a hard night previously and was befuddled, confused, I didn't even look at the number to see who it was calling, I answered and was immediately greeted by my sobbing Mum telling that she and the family knew about the drugs, the women, the drinking, she told me I had two beautiful children who were relying on their Daddy and that they loved me and wanted me home, " come home love, we're all here and no ones judging you, we all love you".

I was so shocked I thought my clandestine lifestyle was only mine to know but no my Mum and family all knew and were hoping I would snap out of it but in reality, it took my Mum's call to make me realise it had to end and it had to end now!

I managed to ride my motorbike home later that morning and was greeted by everyone, I felt so ashamed and tawdry yet I knew deep inside me I had everything I needed here to get me through this and my children needed Daddy more than ever now, they needed the stability amidst the chaos that had become their life!

My universe had collapsed, my life had disintegrated, the absolute centre of my universe for so long, my wife had betrayed me, she gave me no quarter, no second chance didn't even contemplate it, she just wanted out and after being together for nearly twenty years that hurt the most, she tore me apart.

There was no "afterbask" no clarity of thought, no living "without" or even "living within" I was lost and frightened, broken and smashed but I had survived the greatest onslaught I had ever had to face and somehow deep inside me I knew that "The Afterbask" was still glimmering, it might only be an ember but nonetheless it was there.

I had strength of character, I had my children, I had my family and from those foundations great things can be achieved, man is not an island!

Chapter 29: The fog

I moved into my Mum's spare room, it was very difficult to be honest, I loved her to pieces but I hadn't lived at home for over twenty years and had prided myself on my independence and had a very successful career and been incredibly independent for many years forging my own life and career but here I was now a grown man moving back to live with his Mum.

To be honest at the time it was the single best thing move I had made in a long time.

I was a total emotional wreck, walking through fog, if someone even looked at me the wrong way or said something in a slightly aggressive manner I felt as though I wanted to burst into tears. My fitness had suffered terribly over the last few months as I hadn't even been able to workout which in essence was an intrinsic part of my life blood, part of my core foundation and my short-term drug abuse had taken its toll.

I always had an innate and vibrant energy that simply shone out of my aura and many people remarked on it but if they could see me now they wouldn't recognise this shell of a man, grey skin, tired, drawn and to make matters worse I had been diagnosed with clinical depression, me, Mr. Indestructible, Mr. Fitness, Mr. Health, Mr. Energy. Mr. I'm invincible, suffering from clinical depression. If it wasn't so serious I would have laughed as I always thought that people who had clinical depression were weak and yet here was I barely able to get out of bed at 4pm everyday shuffling downstairs and then falling asleep again for another two or three hours.

It was a miserable existence!

It was a miserable experience and yet one I now know I had to go through for it was to be my healing by road to recovery.

My Mum was totally awesome, she looked and fussed after me constantly, sometimes to the extent it would drive me insane and I'd snap at her for reason but I knew she really cared and was pleased to be helping "her little boy" through a very tough time indeed and if it wasn't for my Mum, I would have been homeless!

I had no drive, no focus, no energy, no vision, no income no money, no assets, nothing!

The wicked witch was quite happily living in the marital home at the time until we were able to sell it and I was in no state to contest anything at this time, I couldn't even face a solicitor so basically, she got everything. The £20,000 I was supposed to get from the sale of the house "miraculously" disappeared as "The Weasel" in his one last act of cowardly and low life acts had put a "directors loan" in the company books under my name and all the cash withdrawals he had made to pay for company goods and materials were all marked as cash for Garth, I had no way of proving to the liquidators that this wasn't the case, the slimy bastard had played his cards well and to this day I don't know what I'd do if I ever saw him again.

The words forgive and forget mean just that and it's hard enough with the best will in the world to forgive but once you do it's surprisingly easy to do, but this vile insignificant "person" I can't even call him a man was so underhanded and had no regard for anyone or anything apart from covering his own backside, he didn't even have the morale fibre or courage to face up to his actions and he had been significant in destroying my marriage and my life and my good reputation, my honour code had been violated and I wasn't given the opportunity to put things right.

Chapter 30: Emergence

I'd had enough, it was time to get things together again, it was time to put this behind me and start moving forward again, it was time for the re-emergence of Garth!

A year and a half had gone by, I was training again, I hadn't touched drugs for over a year and in truth I was never an addict, they were simply an easy accessible means of escape and I didn't need them anymore, simple as that!

I could feel my old energy coming back, my children used to come and visit me every single weekend and it was a wonderful time for and also a fantastic bonding period for us again. We had always been incredibly close and the absolute pain of not living under the same roof as my babies, tucking them in at night and waking up to their smiling faces was unbearable I missed them dreadfully but the weekend visits were wonderful and we shared some wonderful moments together and they were as happy to see their Daddy as I was to see them and it was more of an adventure for them because they also got the chance to see their Granny on a regular basis and needless to say my Mum was in her element, bless her.

I sat there pondering my future and simply knew I never wanted to go back into the corporate world again as long as I lived, so what to do.

I started to analyse my skills and experience, the pros and cons little realising at this time I was mapping out my new road map, setting my course for my future.

My brother came to visit me and had the fantastic idea of us both becoming commercial martial arts instructors, it seemed such an outrageous plan but one that really appealed to me as it played to all my strengths and skills without having to think too much which to me at that time was sheer luxury as I could do this almost on auto pilot.

I had trained practically every day of my life (and still do) so this was going to be fun. We approached a gym chain in Islington on the Friday and presented our plan, we were so enthusiastic and had so much energy but I also realised I was using my presentation skills that had served me so well throughout my life, they bought into it straight away and gave us three classes a week starting from that Monday.

The old magic was still there!

Chapter 31: One final slap

My brother and I threw ourselves into the training whole heartedly.

I hadn't trained regularly for a while so my fitness was struggling but once you've got it you never really lose it and "muscle memory" will always prevail, one of the reasons I work out even when I go on holiday which used to surprise many people is the fact that even if you just have a week off from training, let alone two weeks, the loss of strength and fitness isn't worth it, it's too big a hill to climb when you come back, I've always found it's much easier to maintain it and that way you never ever lose it, but I've always personally had an iron discipline and realise that not everyone has.

The classes were an immediate and roaring success and before we knew it we started to have a huge following.

Our classes alone would attract more that thirty people per class which was unheard of then.

It was fun, it was exhilarating and it was keeping me fit and meeting new people on a regular basis. We maintained right from the start that we would also turn this into a social event so after every class we would invite people back to the pub afterwards and we always had a fantastic response. Before I knew it, I had a whole load of new friends and eager students wanting to know "the way of the warrior"!

There's something very different about being a martial arts instructor as opposed to a gym fitness instructor or an aerobics teacher.

As soon as you put on the glorious black belt and step in front of the class there was an instant "respect" it was almost tangible and because I was also held a second Dan even more so. Everyone wants to be a Bruce Lee or Jean Claude van Damme and even the girls wanted to learn to "kick ass", they seemed to realise automatically the blood sweat and tears that went into gaining that belt and believe me we never ever made those classes easy for anyone, if you wanted your belt, you worked bloody hard to gain it. To gain respect you have to respect yourself and if you respect yourself and the effort that went into gaining something it becomes so much more special and it gives you a mental edge that money can never buy, in effect you're taking a toehold in the world of "The Afterbask".

I was in my element, all my years of training, weights and martial arts had forged me a will of iron, I had steel discipline and a fitness and strength level that was unsurpassed and something I take huge pride in even to this day, if you want "The Afterbask" to have clarity of thought to be "without" you had to "walk the walk and talk the talk, not only that you had to lead from the front which to mind was incredibly important.

This was a lesson I learned early on my business life, never give anyone a task or a project that you are unwilling to do or can't do "with knobs on". If you don't know what you're talking about how can you lead with respect and be taken seriously?

So, with this important lesson in mind and bear in mind I'm not a huge man, and I weigh 70kgs not huge but I pack so much dynamism power and strength into the package I can be a formidable physical and mental opponent.

I made up my mind before I started teaching martial arts commercially that there would always be a "head hunter" in the class, someone who wanted to prove how tough they were or someone who hadn't learned respect yet and were ready to decry a lot of what you said by the insane measuring stick that "they were bigger and heavier than me".

I was going to be faster and stronger than anyone who ever came into my class or at the very least as fast and as strong as that person, I'm incredibly proud to say I never let myself down and always lead from the front, it was the only way and by also standing in front of these people with supreme confidence and demonstrating time after time that size meant nothing, respect was quick to come.

I never knew fear in class there was no room for it, I learned years ago while I was training with my sensei and sparring at the dojo, if you showed or felt any fear no matter how big your opponent, one, they would sense it but more importantly you were programming your own mind for "failure" because you were sending it the wrong message.

Feel the fear by all means but don't get swallowed up by it, use it to your advantage, all these things I learned on a daily basis but it wasn't until I started to put my own personal system together did I realise how much experience, technique and knowledge I actually had, and it was all "experimental" real life stuff.

The Lifestyle Guy was being conceptualised "unconsciously" here and everything I had learned and experienced would be part of it, clarity of thought was here, "The Aftterbask" was burning hard and bright my destiny was being unfolded and I was loving it!

Then something very strange happened.
Somewhere along the way my brother started to get very distant, there was a gap growing between us. I wasn't quite sure what was going on but decided against saying anything as it simply wasn't worth rocking the boat and I thought it would just blow over.

I was wrong!

Chapter 32: Betrayed again

From the beginning of us teaching martial arts we had discussed setting up and running a franchise of these awesome classes throughout London and because of my business skills he wanted me to telephone and approach all the London gyms and present our proposal. I was doing a lot of work and starting to make progress and then it happened.

He called me up and asked to meet before for a coffee where he then quite calmly told me that he didn't want to work with me anymore and wanted to go alone.

I was hurt but not surprised, the distance that had been growing between us had been increasing and he was becoming more and more insular almost on a daily basis and to be honest I had had enough of stepping around "egg shells" with him, this was my younger brother after all, we had grown up without any kind of sibling rivalry (or so I thought) I loved him and thought he loved me and now after all that we had been through together and after all we had been through at "The Agency" and with "The Weasel" he was in fact dumping me and dumping me unceremoniously and without preamble.

I accepted it and decided to move on although I did teach a few more classes to finish off.

Betrayal and abandonment might seem like strong words but they're the only word I can think of for how I feel, I had looked after my brother all his life, with spending money, with work and he had been a major part of my married and children's lives and now he plainly wanted nothing to do with me at all.

Strangely enough I thought us being apart might bring us closer again but unfortunately our relationship went from bad to worse and sadly, our relationship would never be the same again!

Chapter 33: The Phoenix arises

So, what to do?

I was finally alone for the first time in my place, no wife to look after no brother to work with, no partners, for the first time in many years I was a "lone warrior" again.

Saddened but nonetheless strengthened by events I've never been a quitter, always a fighter and even though I had been battered and bruised in some of my "fights" even though I had taken punishment of unredeemable pain, smashed, knocked on the floor and even admittedly knocked out cold, I had survived and through it all I had become so much stronger!

I was going to use this strength, the sheer enjoyment of being a martial arts instructor had struck a really happy note within me as it felt so right, "The Afterbask" was there as was clarity of though and I felt strong and motivated and loved being around people and seeing massive changes in them through physical training.

The huge impact I'd had on so many people's lives just by being positive, by being patient, by encouraging and never belittling anyone but also by being educated and knowing what I was talking about.

I had unleashed the inner and outer power of many individuals not just by the physical training but also by the words that I used, words that came to me easily and naturally, I was a natural born leader and I could inspire people, in fact that was a major part of my early success, coupled with my positive outlook, my can-do nature, my happiness and of course the awesome power of "The Afterbask".

So, what to do?

This needed careful thought as I knew what I did next would be the road map I would use for my next career, my next journey, my next adventure!

Eureka!

Clarity of thought was so with me again, I could feel it coursing through my body, I was living "without" again and it was a truly wonderful feeling for I knew that here I was in my power and when I'm in my power or anyone is, massive and wonderful things always happen.

I was going back to college and I was going to become a personal trainer.

All my life I had been into physical exercise, weight training, kickboxing, nutrition and I had been reading Muscle and Fitness since it was originally a black and white magazine and called Muscle Builder. My bookshelves were full of bodybuilding and exercise books, Bruce Lee had been my very first role model and Arnold Schwarzenegger's book "Education of a Bodybuilder" had inspired me at age 19 to set my goals and aspire to greatness this was a completely natural progression I now realise, I had all the knowledge I just needed an official certificate to prove it.

Over the years because people knew I was massively into my physical training I found that a lot of people were actually coming to me for help and advice anyway, particularly when I worked at "The Agency", my influence was quite apparent because at one time I had a whole load of people coming down a local boxing gym with me on a regular basis and I even talked a couple into joining the kickboxing club I belonged to in Kings Cross and I revelled in it, I was the man to ask about anything physical and anything to do with exercise and if I didn't know it, it was easy enough to go to one of my magazines or books within my vast library.

I was also getting into nutrition in a huge way at this time as well and again the bodybuilding books were proving an invaluable source of information to me and I loved the way that by changing my body I was also changing the way I felt about myself, it was empowering it was "The Afterbask".

Achieving the physical challenges I was setting up for myself on a daily basis in the gym or dojo was changing the way my mind worked, it made me realise just how strong the mind is and I was transferring these skills to everyday use easily and effortlessly.

I started to not only research nutrition but experiment with it and to chart how certain foods made me look or feel, how some foods made me feel "heavy" and lethargic and seemed to smooth me out, whereas other foods would make me feel "lighter" and give me masses of energy, it was my proving ground and again I was leading my example.

I discovered a wonderful way of eating many years which I still follow to a certain these days and that method is "food combining", I won't go into too many details here but suffice to say I found it a wonderful way to eat and the feelings of energy and well-being that eating this way brought me were immeasurable.

In fact, during the course of a month eating this way I unintentionally lost a stone in weight (14lbs) without even wanting to, my body was just automatically processing and digesting food easily and naturally and the kickback was "fat loss" and lean weight gain, at one point I had more than half the creative department at "The Company" eating this way and extolling its virtues and benefits and how good they felt.

With hindsight as I've mentioned before which is a truly awesome gift I should have changed careers at this point in my life, but hey, ce la vie!

If I had changed then I now realise, I wouldn't have had the life experiences which have made me the lifestyle expert and person I now am.

The college course proved to be pretty easy if I'm honest and I actually found that I knew more than a lot of my course instructors which was a huge confidence boost for me at the time, it just verified that I really did know what I was talking about, in fact I could have quite easily gone on and become a tutor myself I feel.

But college was great for me and all the knowledge I had accumulated over the years was now proving invaluable and I also made some wonderful friends there as well.

I qualified not only as a fitness instructor but decided to stay on and go the whole "hog" and also qualified as a personal trainer, a fitness and physical assessment assessor, nutritionist and exercise to music teacher, don't ask me about the last one, it seemed like a good idea at the time and I actually needed it because when I was teaching the odd kickboxing class in London a lot of the moves I choreographed were to music and therefore had to prove I had a qualification to do it.

I found that by exercising to a "beat" it was much easier to teach people not only simple moves but also complex ones as they just naturally went with the rhythm, well most of the time although there was the odd exception.

I came out of college full of the joys of life, I now had the necessary qualifications to start moving my life forward in the way I wanted and knew that all the knowledge and skills I thus far accumulated were now going to be put to good use.

Chapter 34: Fortune smiles

Within a week one of the friends I had met at college who was already a personal trainer called me up and said that he was full up and had a potential lady client in Kensington who wanted a personal trainer. He gave me her contact details and I called her straight away, there wasn't a moment to lose!

She sounded lovely and asked me to go around for a chat.

I met "Zsa Zsa" for the first time the following day and we hit it off immediately and she promptly booked me for three sessions a week beginning the following day, I was off and running.

Man, I felt so good that day, everything I had gone through, all the blackness, all the terror, all the fear, the betrayal, all the hurt and pain seemed to disappear and melt into nothingness, all those numerous workouts over the years, all those kickboxing sessions all the hard work at college, all my knowledge, skill and experience were now coming to the fore, clarity of thought and the "The Afterbask" were indeed strong in this one again.

"Zsa Zsa" was a delightful lady, funny, warm, gorgeous and had a real iron will herself and was determined to change her body, a real hard-core attitude which I love in people, if you want to change and the desire is there, I'm your man!

Even though our relationship was completely professional at all times we very quickly became good friends and because she was (I discovered at a slightly later date) a very well-known psychotherapist within the London area also had a very large client base herself.

"Zsa Zsa" was a completely unselfish lady and I was very lucky to have found her for as our relationship grew so did her trust in me and within a short period of time and thanks to her personal referrals I had a wonderful client base of personal training clients around the Kensington, Chelsea, Mayfair and Knightsbridge areas of London, a veritable who's who, it was awesome and I met and trained some truly wonderful people!

Life was good again and like previously, I was now living "without" I was in my power and things were coming to me again almost effortlessly and more importantly I was having enormous fun.

My time with "Zsa Zsa" was to prove invaluable, not only for the contacts she so generously provided and referred me to but she was an incredibly intelligent, knowledgeable, fun and warm hearted lady to be around and I learned an awful lot more "unconsciously" from her than I actually realised at the time and I used to really enjoy my time with her and the workouts I put her through.

I was now a mobile personal trainer and nutritionist and travelling from client to client house to wonderful house on my motorbike on a daily basis and training people within their homes which was a new and novel experience and obviously very different from training in a gym, I had to be constantly creative and adapt to different environments and different scenarios on a daily basis, life was never boring, new challenges, new ways of having to think and train people with very little equipment kept me fresh, enthusiastic and energised, after all I was living the dream.

I also introduced kickboxing routines into a lot of people's programmes and I was truly amazed at how just ordinary housewives would so enjoy beating the hell out of a pair of pads but more importantly I was now beginning to realise I had tapped into something much deeper here, it wasn't just about the exercise anymore for a lot of people.

It was a release, anger management, their own way of letting go and releasing pent up emotions and what I was now beginning to find that as my relationships started to grow and develop with these individuals that all of a sudden I wasn't just a personal trainer or a kickboxing instructor anymore, I was their emotional release.

With me they felt safe and able to let go through physical exercise (just like I had discovered so many years previously) of all their pent-up frustrations and anger and through the fact that I saw many of them on a regular basis I became their "sounding board" not only physically but also verbally, with me they felt safe enough to let go.

This wasn't just isolated incidents, this was across the board, house wives, single ladies and men, company directors, powerful corporate individuals, couples who trained with me, it was universal, everyone seemed to have issues and everyone wanted to not only talk about them, whether it was physical, nutritional or emotional but to also release them.

To them they did it naturally and without prompting because the exercise the feeling of feeling so good, the built-in ability I naturally had to develop, trust, empathy and rapport prompted this emotion, they had to let go, they had discovered they're own "Afterbask"!

To me this was a total revelation and the more I thought about it, it just confirmed what I had known all my life and I knew I was experiencing something special and confirmed that I had a special talent of communication at all levels, that I could communicate on many levels with all kinds of people that I clearly needed to develop, if I could have such a positive impact and influence on a few individuals how wonderful and awesome would it be if I could do it on a much greater level.

This also showed me that the talents, skills, emotions and experiences I had developed through the absolute energising and grounding effects of physical exercise could positively benefit anyone at any level, clarity of thought flowed naturally, "within" became living "without" in short "The Afterbask" was very very real!

The concept of The Lifestyle Guy was germinated and was to take full root within a short period of time I just had to allow the universe, my clarity of thought to percolate a while longer and all would be revealed to me.

Chapter 35: Life coach

If I was going to offer help and advice not only on a physical and nutritional level but also at an emotional level I felt as though I needed to be qualified to do this, for although my life's experiences had served me well and taught me much I wasn't a psychotherapist or a psychologist and I wanted to be able to give them so much more but more importantly I wanted to come from a place of knowledge and authority and enhance and add to what I already offered.

I started to consider and research life coaching and it immediately appealed to me. It was about building relationships, developing not only trust but empathy and rapport.

"The Afterbask" was looking after me wonderfully still and as chance would have it at the time Newcastle University where running correspondence courses for life coaches, how awesome was that.

I enrolled immediately and loved it from the very first course of programmes. It intuitively felt right and just as importantly it made you go deep inside yourself and search out, find and deal with your own personal issues, for there's no way on earth you can help other people if you have unresolved issues.

Again, for me this was cathartic, enlightening, empowering and incredibly exciting and taught me many things about myself and gave me some wonderful tools that would enhance my product, my brand as The Lifestyle Guy.

Yes, through my life coaching, through this process, the universe had automatically "branded me" The Lifestyle Guy was born but was still being developed and would lead me to even more exciting things.

I sailed through the first course and was awarded and received very proudly my certificate in life coaching which still holds pride of place in my portfolio of skills and qualifications.

This led easily and naturally onto the "diploma course" where I had to life coach for real four individuals and present my notes and case studies. Again, I was loving this, I was in my element, I was helping others through their ordeals, challenges and decision making processes, it was a role I was born to and what made it even better was the fact I could use the techniques and strategies I was learning not only on my course subjects but also on my daily personal training clients!

It was wonderful, not only was I taking in the theory I was also putting it to practical use on a daily basis, what better proving ground than real life and what experience, it was a perfect combination.

I sailed through the diploma course.

I was on fire and filled with an energy and enthusiasm that seemed to have no limits. Clarity of thought was constant, living "without" was happening daily, it was so like the early years when everything just flowed and ideas and situations just seemed to materialise for me naturally, this was "The Afterbask" doing its thing.

Chapter 36: The next stage

Like everything new I get into I throw and immerse myself in it completely, it becomes a passion, for I've found over the years that really loving something that I do it becomes joyful and fun and automatically translates into a positive message that people pick up on straight away.

So, I now had a complete system, not just a kickboxing instructor, not just a personal trainer, not just a nutritionist, not just a life coach, I knew automatically with my business skills and life experiences I had something special here and I was about to put the finishing touches to it, I just needed one or two final ingredients to make it the finished product.

Throughout the life coaching course, they kept touching on the words NLP, which for anyone who doesn't know is short for "Neuro Linguistic Programming" and what it is in short is to help people overcome any non-positive thought patterns, behaviours or any thought patterns in essence that have been holding them back in life.

It's a hugely powerful tool for making lasting and dramatic change in your life and an NLP practitioner is trained on how to use those skills in helping people make those lasting changes.

It's about finding out which buttons you've been pushing and which programmes you've been running through your brain over the years and helping you to formulate new programmes and create a few new buttons to push.

Its mind blowing and I wanted some of it!

I researched thoroughly and found what I was looking for, and believe me I wasn't disappointed, I loved it!

Again it involves doing a lot of work on yourself which proved to be very cathartic, powerful and enriching for me personally and I knew instinctively that if this stuff could work so well on me as an add on to what I already offered it would be unbeatable and bring about change on many levels, emotionally, nutritionally and physically, the system was almost complete, I say almost because I felt there was still something missing, ingredient X for a better phrase, something that would help me to install all this properly and professionally and more importantly make sure it was stored in the correctly, I wanted to people to not only feel different after working with me but I wanted to make such a positive and massive difference to them and their lives I wanted them to sound different and to look different as well. I wanted to make such a positive and dramatic change in people that their own friends and family would immediately notice the difference and say "wow, what the hell has happened to you, you look and sound fantastic"!

I basically just needed a "software package" that would help me deliver it something that would "grease the wheels" and make it easy to use and understand.

Hypnotherapy!

Bang, it came to me almost like a thunder clap, the perfect "software package" it would enable me to "install" these wonderful and positive changes in their unconscious minds the part of their minds that actually run their brain, the "navigator" to their pilot, the main computer that controlled every decision you consciously make.

So that was it, ingredient X, the final missing part. I studied and trained hard like everything I enjoy and become passionate about and it was a natural process, something I took to like a "duck to water" and before long I was a fully qualified advanced clinical hypnotherapist.

The list of credits and qualifications alongside my name was growing impressively, however I'm not about titles and qualifications for I knew unlike a lot of "gurus" out there who had learned everything from books all my "learnings" were experiential and I had learned things the hard way, on the job, a grounding and proving ground that can never be replicated.

I had forged my early career, my body and now my mind by my iron discipline, strength of character and powerful will and I was eager to share it with the world at large!

I kept my personal training clients on the go but also decided to set up my own Lifestyle Practice and started to look for office space.

"The Afterbask" was burning beautifully fierce and everything like it had previously before I gave away my power was now coming to me without even trying, I was just putting g the thought out there and things happened.

A close friend of mine who was the creative services director for a large advertising agency offered me free office space in a wonderful area of London called Paddington, it was perfect, the top floor and in a premier location to boot!

I spent some cash and modernised the floor space, I had a very definite idea in my head on how I wanted the place to look and feel. It had to have immediate ambience for it had to create a feeling of "instantly" being comfortable, almost like walking into your front room and relaxing, the room itself had to be able to create "rapport" instant empathy.

I had a wonderful reception area with a wonderful leather settee and very grounding colours, purple and green cushions on black leather, a welcoming wooden floor and a fantastic and tasteful art piece on the wall, I also had wooden doors and half wallpaper on the walls as I wanted to get as far away form "Austere" and "modern" as possible, this had to be a "home from home".

My office itself was wonderful, with the grounding colours theme carried on throughout and as ad added touch I had natural wood blinds on the windows and gorgeous Chinese artefacts and figurines placed tastefully around the room, it was paradise and I loved being there myself.

I knew I had everything right, for the moment I walked through that door, I was empowered, I was happy, I was centred and grounded and it felt wonderful, it touched my soul and made my spirit sing.

My client base soon grew and I was doing wonderful things with people and making some lasting and powerful changes, everything I had learned in the outside world was now coming together.

There was nothing that could phase me, I had practically gone through everything that life could throw at you so there was nobody who threw anything at me that caught me by surprise or caught me unawares and it was here that I finally crafted all my "emotional" techniques to fully complement everything I knew about the body, physical exercise and nutrition, I had even upped my nutritional skills by becoming a "weight management coach" as well and ran many successful ladies groups in my office for weight loss and maintenance without anyone ever having to go on a diet, it was simply a case of "personal desire" and then implementing the required lifestyle changes in bite sized and manageable chunks, simple.

Evolution not revolution!

Most people on the six-week course lost on average about 14lbs and the main thing is kept it off and I still keep in touch with everyone to this day to offer support, I'm not just a here today and gone tomorrow sort of guy, although I never want to be a "crutch" for anyone for if you do, no one ever stands on their own two feet, you haven't "empowered" them you've only made them reliant on you and that's not the result we're after.

Chapter 37: New horizons

My creative services friend at a well-known London advertising agency was also now very interested in what I was doing and after a lengthy conversation as he wanted to implement some major changes within his department invited me into his company to run a Lifestyle review within his company.

This is a major programme that I run for corporates and individuals alike and consists briefly of a psychometric questionnaire which pertinent to that particular individual, this will then highlight any areas of concern within this individual's lifestyle, anger, frustration, depression, feeling down, the fit between work and home life etc etc.

I then get them to fill in a three-day food diary which also gives me and them a complete nutritional analysis and breakdown of their eating habits and how to make positive changes and it also includes a full physical assessment, so like I said a very comprehensive programme.

The reports generated are only for the eyes of the individual and anything highlighted that needs addressing I will do it on a one to one basis.

From these individual reports a global report is then generated which I then discuss with the MD or CEO or department manager on the best way forward.

With my help, he rearranged his department to maximum efficiency and a year later he informed me that profits and morale had rise remarkably. Not only that one of his apple mac operators who I had worked with exclusively had not only lost four stone in weight (112lbs) he had such an attitude change he been promoted and was head of the studio.

Stories like this just fill me with happiness and joy for apart from my workouts nothing puts me in "The Afterbask" quicker than news like this.

Not only that, I had proved unequivocally that only did my system work with individuals it also worked for large companies and groups of people, I had arrived.

I then had the good fortune, or should I say "The Afterbask" helped me bump into my old sensei again who I hadn't seen now for a while, for although I still trained I didn't train with him.

He had always been a huge positive influence on me and had taken me into and out the other side of "the pain barrier" many times in our years ago together. Not only was he my sensei he was my friend and he had shared in all my ups and downs and been there with his words of wisdom and his physically and mentally punishing workouts which always helped to "drive out the demons".

He knew if I needed a "beating" or a chat and many a time after training whilst stretching out on the mats we would put the world to rights, I thoroughly being in his company and he in turn was very pleased to see me as well.

This was becoming a very exciting period of my life, he had just set up a very trendy gym right in the heart of Camden Lock, in fact it was in the middle of Camden market, a huge sprawling converted warehouse over two floors.

It was all brand spanking new and he was like a little kid as he showed me around.

There was the downstairs reception area with a completely empty floors pace behind it as he was deciding whether to install weights or not and I was going to prove not only beneficial but also influential in this key area but didn't know it at the time.

Going up the stairs lead to a wonderful healthy food and juice bar and off to the left was a meditation, yoga or tai Chi room. To the right was another large floor space which was the "dojo" proper and just behind that the alternative therapy rooms, acupuncture, massage etc.

It was lovely, the perfect blend of harmonics for mind, body and soul and it was placed in one of the vibrant parts of London.

I started to go up there and train on a daily basis and it was just so exhilarating to be training in an environment like this again and the one of the best things about the place was that sensei had taken many of his long standing students with him from the Kings Cross club, every time I went up there it was like an old boys reunion with so many faces from the old days it was just like "the good old days" and in truth in many ways it was, I was in a safe and exciting place and amongst friends, I was truly enjoying being in my power again being in "The Afterbask" and the was very quick to reward you as a consequence.

It was just so awesome to be there training hard will all the lads and Sensei again and there were also quite a few famous faces there as well due to the location which made it doubly exciting.

It was apparent after a few weeks training up there that my fitness levels and endurance were incredibly high and sensei besides awarding me my black belt many years previously gave me the greatest accolade he had ever given me when he remarked on how fit I was now. He was in fact so impressed by my fitness that he had me training his senior level black belt instructors in body conditioning.

You will have to have trained for as long as me and in that environment to realise the true significance of what that meant, these were hard fit men and I had been asked to train them and by sensei in person, I was ecstatic!

I was truly buzzing and living the dream but things just got better and better as they naturally would if you're being true to yourself, it can happen in no other way.

I was then asked of If I would become their resident Lifestyle Manager and offer my services to all their clients which I was more than happy to do and I did Lifestyle Assessments, which included emotional well-being and nutrition to quite a few well know faces along the way, this was like a dream come true, a successful business in Paddington where I worked three days a week, I still some personal training clients and now this.

Sensei was quick to realise my knowledge of personal training and equipment and I was asked my advice and asked to help choose the equipment for the downstairs gym which in turn lead into some personal training on site there as well.

This man was so generous and one huge lesson I learned from sensei many years previously is to "be generous" and give unconditionally, he was one of "the hardest men" I knew, not only a British kickboxing champion but also had numerous European tiles as well as wait for it…. being a World Champion and he was wise beyond his years.

Perhaps now you can understand why I held this man in such high esteem.

Chapter 38: opportunity knocks

Then one day a "golden opportunity" presented itself, or should I say "The Afterbask" provided one.

Sensei was visited by an Evening Standard journalist and her husband who also happened to be a freelance writer of some importance.

This was exciting!

Nigel who was the husband wanted to lose three stone in weight (42lbs) and his wife was then going to write an article for The London Evening Standard called "Fat to Fit in 8 weeks" as he went through and documented his progress on a dally basis.

Rep for punishing rep, every kick and every blow of his kick boxing workouts, and more importantly to my mind his nutrition.

I had learned over the years that as important as regular exercise is you will never see the results you crave if you don't change and adapt your eating habits as well, I firmly believe that nutrition is 80% of any training programme, end of story!

To illustrate this point I always like to hold up a "natural body builder" as opposed to one pumped up on steroids as a prime example of this. Love them or loathe them there is no escaping the fact that they are world class nutritionists and can use their food with such uncanny skill that can they can be at a particular body weight or a body fat percentage on a given date which I've always been incredibly impressed with, this was a science and you had to have at least a basic understanding of nutrition or food if you are going to make any progress at all.

I sat down with Nigel and questioned him at length about his goals, his health and the reason why he wanted to lose so much so quickly although it was fairly obvious as he was hugely overweight and he wouldn't mind me saying that either.

I went over his lifestyle, exercise and eating habits with him and his wife meticulously and it made me chuckle as he began to tell me how he wanted to go about it, with the plan he had in mind he would kill himself within two weeks, it just wasn't sustainable. I then proceed to tell him how he would be trained in which particular manner and what he could and couldn't eat, this was obviously incredibly important to him, he had realised as had his wife that if something wasn't done now it would just escalate and let's not forget his pride was on the line here, not only was he going to have before and after pictures taken with his shirt off he was also going to feature in a major London newspaper!

They left a happy couple with the intent of coming back the following day for the before pictures and then I would go through his training and nutrition programme with him.

Sensei was feeling a little doubtful of the end result as he had never attempted anything like this before but I assured him that this was "bread and butter" to me and to be truthful I really relished the challenge. I had no doubt in my mind that this could be done as I had previously run so many weight management programmes for groups and individuals with great success, this was going to be fun and the ideal proving ground for my entire system, this was where the "Circle of Trinity" was born which would include for the first time all my technique and strategies together, mind body, soul, nutrition, well-being and physical exercise, this was going to be my showcase and because it was such a public event it had to succeed.

Chapter 39: Circle of trinity

I worked out a training programme overnight and took sensei through it the following day. He would be totally responsible for all his kickboxing sessions for after all he was the master and I would cover every other aspect of his training.

Nigel was coming in later with his wife for his brief and first topless photo shoot.

Sensei and I then took Nigel through his schedule and training programme starting from tomorrow and in fairness he never baulked or flinched, he was ready.

I knew I had to be very careful with this man and I had given it a huge amount of thought, he had to be broken down and rebuilt not only physically but I recognised straight away that this would be a mental challenge as well. I had to change his very thought processes and just as importantly he had to recognise that it was his battle, his personal challenge, I could give him the physical exercise and mental tools that he needed but ultimately, he held his own destiny in his hands and this was a point I played on over and over again.

And so, it began, eight weeks of pure purgatory for this man, he had to achieve a result, three stone (42lbs) in eight weeks, I personally knew he wouldn't achieve that particular weight loss in that period without causing him some damage but also recognised with the correct eating plan we could make significant and lasting changes.

I outlined and wrote out a completely new and comprehensive eating plan for him but at the same time didn't make it so drastic that he would crave the foods he loved, he was allowed a weekly treat, I just had to change the order, sequence, timings and portions of the food he was already eating.

This was an intrinsic part of my "Circle of Trinity" little and often and in his case no starchy carbs after 4pm as this would be primarily stored as fat.

I've learned over the years that if you take out a favourite food from a person's lifestyle all of a sudden, they start to crave it and eventuality it becomes what I call "forbidden fruit" and when something is "forbidden" guess what, the craving intensifies.

Nigel was awesome, he turned up every single day on schedule and some days I would see the weariness in his body as he dragged his "sorry carcass" up those stairs, this was when I knew I had to fortify his mental strength, where I had to play little games with him and let him tap into his inner strength unconsciously.

On days like this I would take him for a coffee and "chat". I would tell him how proud I was of him and how normal men wouldn't be able to do what he was actually doing let alone do it every day, I then suggested a walk which then turned into a speed walk which then turned into a jog and before you know it he was ready to hit the weights.

I was constantly reframing things for him not looking as things as challenges but as achievements, every tool, technique and strategy I had used to bring myself back from the brink was pulled out of the bag for I knew they were effective and that they worked.

He was beginning to feel stronger mentally and physically on a daily basis and was now enjoying his new eating patterns as they were actually giving him much more energy as well, it was lovely to see these changes in him and we were also becoming good friends.

He admitted to me later and also in his article that on some days he just felt a "deep loathing" towards me because he knew what was going to happen but as the changes became more and more apparent he actually looked forward to seeing me, which was huge progress.

Chapter 40: Result

The eight weeks came to an end surprisingly quickly, the photographer arrived and Nigel was stripped to the waist and ready.

He looked magnificent!

We hadn't lost the entire three stone (42lbs) as I knew we wouldn't, it would have killed him but you know what, we came spectacularly close, he had lost 34lbs a HUGE achievement.

He was ecstatic, over the moon and the article was published and I was featured in a London newspaper in a very prominent article, I had succeeded, sensei was happy, Nigel was ecstatic as was his wife and I was feeling very satisfied indeed.

Nigel still trains to this day and on the many occasions when I've spoken with him he's credited me solely with changing his entire life and the way he approaches things. He continued his weight loss and is now so trim I hardly recognise him.

I now had a system that was proven and tested in the fires of real life but I was about to also take a step in a slightly different direction.

When you have clarity of thought and truly living "without" everything flows, I had proved it in the past when everything came so easily and effortlessly and now it was repeating itself, "The Afterbask" was my constant companion again and I didn't just need a workout to access it, although I must admit it shines, glows and pulsates even stronger after a workout.

Chapter 41: Personal safety

I still had a few select clients that I was doing personal training and kickboxing sessions with and one evening I was training one of lady clients at her home who had a senior position at Barcap in London's Canary Wharf and was also head of the women in business networking group within the organisation.

She thoroughly enjoyed her kick boxing sessions and used them mainly as "stress relief" to get rid of any anger or frustration she may have been feeling and it always had a very positive and empowering effect on her and she suggested that I go into the company and do a workshop on self-defence for women.

Now this immediately intrigued me as it wasn't anything I had thought about previously but I was instantly catapulted back into time when I first moved to London from the North of England.

Obviously, this was a very stressful time for me as I was still a teenager just 19, and had to leave not only the sanctity of a small town where everyone knew everyone else but also all my boyhood friends, and to make matters worse we moved into a high-rise block of flats which was situated in a very notorious area of NW London, an urban nightmare to say the least!

It took me quite a while to settle down and feel confident in this environment as you may well imagine but as I found my first job and started to make friends it gradually became easier and always being a confident person I soon found my feet and didn't feel quite as threatened as I did originally. But don't get me wrong, this was a rough neighbourhood and bad things happened all the time, you had to constantly have your wits about but I found, and on reflection I think it's because I always outwardly projected my confidence, "The Afterbask" of course I was never ever threatened.

Unfortunately, my family didn't fare as well and my younger sister was "mugged" as they used to call it then, three times by the same youth and the frustrating thing was even though the police knew who he was and he had a "wrap sheet" as long as your arm they couldn't touch him as he always had an alibi and unless they caught him in the act there was little they could do.

I remember being a very angry young man driving around for hours trying to find this guy so I could give him a beating, I was so frustrated and angry that he could terrorise my sister like this and get away with it.

To make matters worse it wasn't long after that my dad was walking home from a night shift at the local hospital when someone approached him asking him for a light for his cigarette, as my dad obligingly reached into his pocket for the lighter this guy just pulled out a knife and without saying a word stabbed him and calmly walked off into the night!

Again, the police could do nothing and again I felt a helpless anger, rage and frustration!
All this came flooding back to me as I was asked to do this workshop and I readily agreed for I thought to myself if I could prevent someone else's Dad or Sister from ever being attacked it was well worth it, it was too late for my family but not for someone else.

I spent about a month thinking about this and how I wanted to present it and started gathering together as much information as I could with a close friend of mine at the time who also happened to be a Metropolitan policeman with over thirty years' experience and his insight and knowledge was invaluable.

I instinctively realised that this wasn't going to be a "self-defence" programme as to my mind that brings up the wrong connotations, it means that something has happened out of your control and you've become a "victim" , I much preferred the idea of safety "through awareness" and not getting into that situation in the first place, although I did add what I now call a few "funky moves" that required no strength or special technique that anyone could use regardless of size to "buy themselves two seconds" to get to a place of safety, and as an added bonus and to finish off the session on a "physical high" now affectionately referred to as "The Afterbask" I also included some dynamic kicking and punching techniques.

I was also incredibly lucky because Nigel the journalist introduced me to a freelance writer who had been attacked a few months earlier in Camden and had been unfortunately beaten up quite badly and she readily agreed to come and cover the workshop and if she liked it would print it in The London Evening Standard.

The workshop was an astounding success and incredibly well received and as good as her word the article was printed and I had appeared in a prominent London newspaper once again, how good was that!

Word spread and the workshops have now become very popular and I have presented to major companies and advertising agencies not only in London but also nationally.

This was also the beginning of something else as in every workshop I talked more and more about body language and the message that you're "unconsciously" sending out and as more and more ladies were approaching me asking if I did any workshops on body language.

I didn't at the time but it definitely made sense so therefore another workshop was added to The Lifestyle Guy arsenal which is a half day course centred around body language, rapport building, essential communication skills, eye movement and the different modalities that individuals operate in and how to recognise those signals and be able to communicate much more effectively with not only your work colleagues but also use these essential skills in your everyday life as well.

The Lifestyle Guy is a grand title that simply encompasses all my lifetime skills, my business experience, management techniques, kick boxing, personal training, nutrition, life coaching, NLP and hypnotherapy and puts them all under one succinct umbrella.

It also utilises all the techniques, skills and strategies I used to pull myself out of the darkness and make my life good again.

Feel free to dip in and out of this book as a means of empowerment, enjoy the joys and triumphs I felt throughout my life, and share in some of the bleaker times but most of all use it to find your own path to your own particular "Afterbask" and find the true path to your power and destiny!

Mirror Mirror On The Wall...

So, as my life transitioned and I began to "reflect" on my experiences it seemed an appropriate time to really find out what the "magic formula" was that really helped me to turn my life around.

I knew that being physically fit and working out on regular basis was a huge part of my journey, challenging not only my mind but also my body to push even further than I ever thought possible but I was also beginning to realise that as big a part as it played in my life it was no greater than the sum of all its parts, namely the way I felt "mentally" and how organising my life to suit my purpose and following my own ideals and not dancing to the tune of others was incredibly empowering. Setting goals for myself, setting time aside to plan and think, organising my day to suit my purpose and nobody else's.

Then I thought about the part that my "emotions" had played in my life, how at times during those significant highs nothing seemed insurmountable, nothing was impossible and I proved it to myself over and over again as every task and goal I set myself I exceeded using the endorphin high from my exercise sessions as the catalyst I need to further fuel my ambitions.

Yet I also realised that when I plummeted to those almighty lows, the endorphin high and the physical challenges were just not strong enough to help me heal, I need something else, I needed to go deeper.

How do I deal with the anger, the sadness, the fear, the guilt, the depression and anxiety?

So, I began to work on my emotions using the very same strategies I share with you in this book and self-same strategies I've shared with hundreds of individuals.

The three mirrors concept has been shaped, formulated, tried and tested not only in my own life but with other people as well. The more I worked with individuals and groups I realised their "inner reflections" the mirror they were the most reluctant to look into was always the place to begin working with them.

By looking into that mirror no matter how difficult or painful, be it physical, mental or emotional was the first brave step in beginning to achieve the lifestyles they'd always dreamed about.

I then then devised the three mirrors test which will pinpoint the exact mirror or mirrors you're avoiding, address the issues, basically shining a light on your inner fears and giving you the tools, techniques and strategies you've always wanted to move your life forward.

So, my friend, it's time to be brave, step up to the mirror and tell me which mirror are avoiding and why?

Let's do this!

Chapter 42: The physical you…The temple of your power!

If only more people would take up some form of physical exercise and experience the awesome benefits that being in shape and physically fit can bring you the world would be a much better place for it in more ways than one.

Being fit helps to keep you healthy, it strengthens your heart; it improves your circulation and helps your lungs and blood oxygenate your body in a more efficient manner.

The amount of people I see nowadays that could benefit immeasurably from being fitter is mind blowing! I see youngsters, teenagers and people barely in their 30's or 40's who are not only overweight but can't even walk upstairs without getting out of breath, people who can't carry shopping bags, young people with back or shoulder problems going on medication and to hospitals on a regular basis when most of their ills are caused by massive inactivity and poor nutrition and not even realising it's their own inactivity and lack of knowledge that is the prime cause of their downfall.

People eating total crap from an early age and thinking it's ok and then wondering why their arteries are seizing up and why they are starting to have heart or respiratory problems but worst of all they accept it as part of growing older or just LIFE!!!!

How awful is that?

I'm not for one second saying here that exercise is the panacea for everything that is bad in your life and making you

101

feel ill or caused your health problems but I am saying that exercise on a regular basis will definitely improve or even stem the cause of all the above problems if you decide to make positive changes NOW!

Exercise makes you physically stronger, it improves your appearance it helps you function more efficiently and best of all to my mind at least it imbibes you with a feeling of supreme self confidence that translates into everything that you do in life.

I discovered the powerful benefits of physical exercise early on in my life when I first moved to London to be exact and I still remember the experience so vividly.

I was 20 years old and had just given up smoking 20 cigarettes a day (cold turkey I might add) and had begun to realise the damage I had done to my body in my years of smoking. My lung capacity was nowhere near where it should have been, I noticed I was struggling to run and down escalators and as a 20-year-old I didn't have the best physique around either!

So, I decided there and then that something had to be done! I've always been proactive so the first thing I did was go find a gym and as luck would have it there was a terrific gym at the time in Bloomsbury Square part of London called "Ravelles" and it advertised itself literally everywhere in those days, and seemingly everywhere you turned there was a poster for "Ravelles" with a picture of a confident looking athletic man smiling benevolently down at you almost saying, "this too could be you!"

As I found out later this chap was called Ray and actually worked at the gym and was a knowledgeable and friendly amateur bodybuilder who used to compete at the time and he ran and managed the gym as far as I can remember with another guy called Patrick.

The thing I really liked about the gym as well as it being well laid out with a great range of equipment was the fact that it made up and served protein shakes as well, which was a terrific way to refuel yourself after a strenuous workout.

Apart from having a dabble with weights at a local weightlifting club up north I'd never really picked up a weight in earnest before but from my very first induction I was hooked and discovered how very quickly you can get in shape if you put your mind to it no matter which form of exercise you decide to do yourself.

And this is the key to everyone's fitness, find something that you personally like to do and then stick at it! Consistency and dedication is the key to anything you wish to achieve in life and exercise and getting in shape is no exception to the rule.

I loved the feeling of exercise and how it made me feel and all of a sudden, the American bodybuilding magazines I'd been reading since a young man were beginning to make real sense, as Arnold made famous in the film Pumping Iron "the pump" was indeed an awesome experience and I began to understand how you could become "addicted" to exercise, in a good way of course.

I never wanted a bodybuilders physique or to compete but I knew almost instinctively that I wanted to be the best that I could possibly become physically as I could feel the benefits already.

So, began my life's journey into physical exercise and as you know from previous chapter I also got heavily into kickboxing over the years as well and successfully managed to combine the training regimens with great success.

One of the added benefits of training I'd like to add are the keys it opens to your inner mind, the keys to your inner power, the keys to every limiting belief or personal barrier that has ever been erected in your life the keys to the temple of your power.

By surpassing your efforts in the gym every time you train or surpassing previous lifts or simply challenging yourself to do something that you haven't previously attempted before is incredibly powerful and get this, even if you don't succeed in the task of attempting something you've never done before is also just as empowering and turns on a switch inside your head that enables you to push yourself further than you ever thought possible not only in the gym but in everything you do in life and business as well. I know, I did it and taught hundreds of other individuals over the years to do the same with their lives.

Accessing your power, where to start?

Exercise is not difficult and it's not mysterious so for a kick off stop reading every piece of crap you see about exercise, high intensity vs low intensity, low cardio vs high cardio and simply pick something that you PERSONALLY enjoy doing and just start doing it, it's as simple as that.

Try to exercise a minimum of three times weekly and for beginners i.e. if you haven't exercised for years, on medication or are new to exercise always check with a doctor first to make sure everything's ok in your world.

Words of advice, if you don't know how to do an exercise properly either get advice from a fitness professional, read a fitness magazine or better still and highly recommended by yours truly, watch a YouTube video.
Again, I would suggest watching the video or reading the article several times and pay strict attention to exercise form at all times as this will prevent any chances of injury.

My recipe for success let's get started!

Now if you're really unfit I would simply suggest just doing two minutes a day for the first two weeks then gradually build up by adding a minute a week until you're exercising twenty minutes a week (remember, twenty is plenty).

Get yourself a timer or if you have a smart device download an exercise interval timer.

Week 1:
Four exercises:
Star jumps – Press ups – Running on the spot – Floor crunches
(if you're not strong enough to do full press ups don't worry, just get on your knees and do them from there until you do get strong enough)

Set your exercise timer for 20 seconds of continuous exercise and 10 seconds of active rest (this where you will walk up and down for ten seconds as opposed to collapsing in a heap on the floor) this is very important as you do not want to stop dead in your tracks ever.

Begin:
Star jumps for 20 seconds nonstop, rest for 10 seconds
Press up for 20 seconds nonstop, rest for 10 seconds
Running on the spot (knees high) for 20 seconds nonstop, rest for 10 seconds
Floor crunches for 20 seconds nonstop, then rest for 10 seconds.

FINISH.

Congratulations you have now succeeded on exercising continually for 2 x minutes!

I bet you didn't think two minutes could feel so tough yet so invigorating, did you?

Week 2:
Six exercises:
Star jumps – Press ups – Running on the spot – Floor crunches – Squats - Plank

Begin:
Star jumps for 20 seconds nonstop, rest for 10 seconds
Press up for 20 seconds nonstop, rest for 10 seconds
Running on the spot (knees high) for 20 seconds nonstop, rest for 10 seconds
Floor crunches for 20 seconds nonstop, then rest for 10 seconds
Squats for 20 seconds nonstop, rest for 10 seconds
Plank for 20 seconds nonstop, then rest for 10 seconds

FINISH.

Congratulations you have now succeeded on exercising continually for 3 x minutes!

Week 3:
This is now where we start to push just a little.

Eight exercises:
Star jumps – Press ups – Running on the spot – Floor crunches – Squats – Plank – Burpees – Floor crunches

Begin:
Star jumps for 20 seconds nonstop, rest for 10 seconds
Press up for 20 seconds nonstop, rest for 10 seconds
Running on the spot (knees high) for 20 seconds nonstop, rest for 10 seconds
Floor crunches for 20 seconds nonstop, then rest for 10 seconds
Squats for 20 seconds nonstop, rest for 10 seconds
Plank for 20 seconds nonstop, then rest for 10 seconds
Burpees for 20 seconds nonstop, rest 10 seconds
Floor crunches for 20 seconds nonstop, rest 10 seconds

FINISH.

Congratulations you have now succeeded on exercising continually for 4 x minutes!

You should be really huffing and puffing by now, this is a good sign as long as you don't feel weak or dizzy.

Stay within the parameters I've instructed and don't try to add too much too soon as this is a guaranteed recipe for disaster.

Week 4:
Ten exercises:
Star jumps – Press ups – Running on the spot – Floor crunches – Squats – Plank – Burpees – Floor crunches – Lunges - Burpees

Begin:
Star jumps for 20 seconds nonstop, rest for 10 seconds
Press up for 20 seconds nonstop, rest for 10 seconds
Running on the spot (knees high) for 20 seconds nonstop, rest for 10 seconds
Floor crunches for 20 seconds nonstop, then rest for 10 seconds
Squats for 20 seconds nonstop, rest for 10 seconds
Plank for 20 seconds nonstop, then rest for 10 seconds
Burpees for 20 seconds nonstop, rest 10 seconds
Floor crunches for 20 seconds nonstop, rest 10 seconds
Lunges for 20 seconds nonstop. Rest for 10 seconds
Burpees for 20 seconds nonstop, walk around for at least 30 seconds

FINISH.

Congratulations you have now succeeded on exercising continually for 5 x minutes!

Keep this exercise programme up for a month then in month two repeat the entire sequence twice so you're exercising for 10 minutes a day, then in month three repeat the entire sequence again three times so you're now exercising for 15 minutes a day and finally in month four repeat the entire sequence four times till you're exercising 20 minutes a day.

I bet by now you will have surprised even yourself with not only how much fitter and alive you actually feel in just five minutes a day but how much more energy you actually have!

Job done and well done you've begun your journey into feeling twenty years younger!

This exercise routine is just a guideline, if you like running use the same formula, sprint for 20 seconds then jog for 10 seconds or if you prefer swimming swim hard for 20 seconds then coast for 10 seconds working whichever routine you prefer but building p up over a period of a month exactly as my schedule.

The important thing here is to simply get active and do something on a daily basis until it becomes second nature.

Strengthening the pillars of your temple!
By now you should really be feeling powerful, strong, invigorated and yearning for more.

Here's my suggested programme for training at home for you to follow but please do whatever you enjoy doing as this is only a guideline. Perhaps you might like to go outside and sprint for 20 seconds then walk for 10 seconds, or maybe step up and down on a park bench for 20 seconds then rest for ten seconds, swim hard for 20 seconds then swim more easily for 10 seconds, the choice is yours.

My suggested training programme: (20-minute exercise)

1) Star jumps 20 seconds then 10 seconds' active rest (walking around)
2) Floor crunches 20 seconds then 10 seconds' active rest (walking around)
3) Running on the spot 20 seconds then 10 seconds' active rest (walking around)
4) Sit ups 20 seconds then 10 seconds' active rest (walking around)
5) Squat with jump 20 seconds then 10 seconds' active rest (walking around)
6) Press ups 20 seconds then 10 seconds' active rest (walking around)
7) Floor crunches 20 seconds then 10 seconds' active rest (walking around)
8) Lunges 20 seconds then 10 seconds' active rest (walking around)
9) Plank 20 seconds then 10 seconds' active rest (walking around)
10) Burpee 20 seconds then 10 seconds' active rest (walking around)

The principle for my Twenty is Plenty is very simple, just keep adding one more exercise every week and one more section of 20 seconds on and ten seconds off until you're exercising continually for 20 minutes.

Or if you like to run or swim ad one more lap or each week until you're doing twenty minutes.

Remember... Twenty's Plenty!

Chapter 43: Sound nutrition...Don't build your temple on a foundation of sand!

Wanting to lose weight, tone up, get in shape and feeling healthy might seem like you have to climb an unassailable mountain sometimes!

But getting healthy and eating a sound, fun and nutritious diet isn't as hard as you may think.

The first thing to do when you start off on any "get healthy plan" is to forget anything you've ever read about diets and the "miracles" they can perform, that's all utter rubbish and just designed to part you with your hard-earned cash and lead you to believe that there's such a thing as a "magic bullet" that will miraculously give you the body and healthy lifestyle you've always wanted.

Diets don't work!

Or let me put it another way, "diets do work" for the six to eight weeks you're on them, but at the end of that period once you've started to look and feel fab, you run out of instructions!

Eeek! What do I eat now, what's next, and before you know it, you slip back into your old eating habits, because that's all you know, and before you know it, you've gained back the weight you lost plus another 28 lbs on top! GUARANTEED!

It was while I was in advertising that I began to realise the importance of good sound nutrition and the benefits it could provide.

I wasn't actually a nutritionist at this time but preferred to what I call **"dabble"** and was already heavily into my training on a daily basis.

I was always into body building from an early age and one of my early models was the Governor of California a.k.a. Arnold Schwarzenegger.

All the bodybuilders were always talking about the importance of nutrition and how it was even more important than the training itself in many ways, because if you didn't give the body the fuel or building blocks it needed you might as well be building a **"house on sand"**.

Even though I grasped the basic concept I didn't really understand it and just decided to start eating more protein as I thought this was paramount to my success in achieving my bodybuilding and strength goals of the time.

Even though I did make a few gains I never really made the spectacular gains that I wanted to.

After leaving the world of advertising and moving into kickboxing instruction and then personal training I really began to start noticing that different foods had different effects on the way that I felt and also on the way I looked so I began to start "experimenting" myself.

It was then that I noticed the effect of having a "balanced" diet and what a major effect it had on improving not only my performance but also my concentration levels.

Over a period of about nine years working as a Lifestyle Manager I formulated my own weight management programme which also centered around and incorporated various powerful techniques which also utilised the mind and explored our personal relationship with food.

The results I started having with clients was outstanding and also my knowledge of "sports nutrition" and being a weight management coach enabled me to not only condition the black belts instructors at a club where I was based but I was also able to increase their stamina for competition due to better nutrition.

The bottom line is this, exercise is good and should be an integral part of any healthy lifestyle but to really see and feel the changes you want in yourself and in your body, you have to have a very close look at what you're putting in as fuel!

The bottom line ...
or as I prefer to call it, healthy eating plan is to eat to suit your own particular personality and lifestyle and you mustn't ever feel that you are depriving yourself!

It's incredibly important to enjoy your food and to enjoy your life and if you're feeling miserable all the time due to deprivation it's never ever going to work and you'll just make the people around you miserable as well.

People who go on diets deprive themselves of all their favourite food and start to eat "bland" unappetizing food, food that they don't enjoy, so after a set amount of time you will drift back to your old eating habits.

When you do go on a diet it's very easy to get carried away with the results as you will find in the first two weeks that your body burns up glucose quite quickly and the initial weight loss is quite significant.

Unfortunately, this loss can't be sustained and the weight loss starts to slow down because the body then has the more difficult job of breaking down complex molecules fat stores and your weight loss will dwindle to almost nothing.

This is when most people feel discouraged and give up, you've done everything right and suddenly you don't appear to be losing any more weight.

Weight loss and weight maintenance isn't just about consuming fewer calories. Exercise releases endorphins which will cheer you up and also help to alleviate stress.

Don't make losing weight the single aim and goal in your life and forget about the scales and weighing yourself, try to look at a more holistic picture imagining how you're going to look and feel and more importantly how you are feeling and how your clothes are feeling on your body!

Chapter 44: Emotional security - strengthening the foundations of your temple!

If exercise is the key to your physical well-being then emotional security is surely the foundations on which your temple of inner power is built. Without the emotional security, we all need in our lives we are just like rudderless ships caught up in the raging torrent of life's dramas and in a modern society which is seemingly fixated on perfection (a concept that doesn't exist even in nature) an ideal of perfection which can never be achieved it's no wonder that more and more people are suffering from stress related symptoms like anxiety, depression, anger, sadness, fear and guilt.

Social media doesn't help with retouched photographs of people bearing no resemblance to themselves even in real life and the epidemic of desperately wanting to be "liked" on social media platforms more people are beginning to feel inadequate and unable to cope.

Comparing yourself to others is one of the worst forms of "self-torture" that I can possibly imagine and yet millions of us are doing it on a daily basis. Our inner voices telling us we're not as good at parenting or that particular celebrity or we don't have a body like the person on television or we don't appear as confident as our ideal role model. Well let me tell you, even your ideal role model is not perfect and have their own particular problems and worries.

Every single person on this planet have their own individual hang ups but the biggest difference in those people and you is the fact they have systems in place to help them cope and deal with their own fears and insecurities and take massive action on a daily basis to ensure that things happen and they continue to improve and be successful.

Life really is not a rehearsal and unless you get good at living your own life and not trying to live the ideals of another person's life you will be forever insecure guaranteed!

But all is not lost and here I'm going to give you some practical tips and advice if you practice on a daily basis for twenty minutes a day will have a massive, lasting and positive impact on your emotional well-being and security.

1. Natural Herbal Remedies:
St. John's Wort
Although often easily accessible from your GP, there are many well-established reasons why taking an antidepressant drug to deal with stress is not a particularly smart move. However, there is absolutely no reason why you should do so because St John's wort is widely believed to provide exactly the same benefits as leading antidepressant brands like Prozac without the side-effects.
Indeed, in some countries in Europe (particularly Germany), St John's wort is prescribed as a treatment for anxiety, stress and depression far more commonly than antidepressants for this exact reason.

2. Physical Activity:
These days life is busy: with deadlines and meetings and traffic, it is difficult to find time for your own care. You begin ignoring your body, and slowly signs of stress start showing on your body.

It becomes all-important to undo the harm and be prepared to confront the consequences.

Doing physical activity for twenty - a day could undo several of the adverse effects of stress. Each day physical activity not only makes you look and feel good and even lose a few extra pounds. It can also make your life less trying.

3. Using Music:

Music is a Healer.

Instinctively we turn to music to unwind and to create a favourable surrounding. Delicate and calming music does a good deal for our frazzled nerves. It washes away the weariness of a busy day.

Music therapy as a healing science is advancing in popularity. Consider the following to understand why music is gaining the attention of healers the world over.

1. Music aids you in sleeping better: In a study of elderly individuals with sleep related troubles, it was reported that listening to Classical and New Age music helped 96% of them to sleep better.

4. Positive Self Talk:

It's very easy to get caught up in the negativity of people around you, but if you can implement these four little steps, you'll find yourself having a great day that will rub off on those around you.

Try these simple techniques to bring a little joy into your day:
1. Wake up with a smile on your face. How many of us wake up and groan at the thought of the day ahead? Tomorrow morning try doing something a little different.
• Set your alarm five minutes earlier than normal. • As you wake up, luxuriate in the warmth and softness of your bed. • Smile to yourself to set your inner mood. • Before you get out of bed, think of five things you're grateful for.

5. Focus on You:

Do you feel like something is missing from your life? Learning to focus on you, instead of others, may be the key you've been seeking!

If you find that you're comparing yourself to others and coming up short, it's time to stop that destructive habit. Comparisons get you nowhere. Rather than leading to positive improvements, they only cause you pain and discontent.

6. Use Affirmations:
One of the best ways to reinforce our positive feelings towards ourselves and to reduce the impact of any negative feelings is through the use of daily affirmations.

Affirmations are just short, positive and personal statements about yourself and/or about your desired outcomes for specific areas of your life. For example, you may use an affirmation to help you remain calm when making presentations at work, such as, "I am calm, confident and relaxed as I deliver my presentation with authority, composure and self-assurance."

7. Time Management:
Let's face it, no-one lies in their death bed wishing that they had spent more time at the office...

You need to treat each and every day as though you were on a special mission – get in, get the job done and get out again!

8. Develop a Stress Management Plan:
A stress management plan does not necessarily require a lot of time and energy. Many times, it is just making a commitment to reduce the level of stress in your life, by taking a few small, but meaningful, steps toward improving your overall health and well-being.

A good place to begin your stress management plan is by identifying 5 activities that you really enjoy participating in. These can be anything from reading a good book, to taking a long walk on the beach.

9. Laughter is Good for You:
Anatomy of Illness written by Norman Cousins is a book based on the true story of how this man treated his own painful illness. Cousins had a theory that there was more to the old saying; Laughter is the best medicine, than many people realize.

In modern times society has come to understand that stress has a negative impact on both physical and mental health. What is not as commonly understood is that laughter has many positive health benefits, which can counteract the negative effects of the stress response.

Everyday day of our lives we're making constant decisions, some of these are made consciously i.e. "get in the car", "let's go shopping", "get ready for bed" etc., and sure enough as you make these decisions, the body will follow suit.

But at the back of our minds in our unconscious, we are also constantly making decisions that will influence our everyday lives, and probably in a much more significant manner.

This is the part of our brain that really does govern our lives, the "navigator" as opposed to the "pilot" of our conscious mind, the part that drives and directs us and it is in this part of our mind that every decision we make influences our every waking and sleeping seconds. It is the inner voice that we use constantly to talk to ourselves, and depending on how we have conditioned this part of our mind over the years we are always listening to it!

So, if you are forever berating yourself, or telling yourself "you can't do this" or you "can't do that", sure enough, your unconscious mind will convey that message to your conscious mind and you will inevitably follow through, either in a positive manner or a negative manner.

If you think, "you can" you can! If you think, "you can't" you can't! as Henry Ford was famously reported saying, It's as simple as that! So, wouldn't it make sense to completely re-programme the software that is your brain and talk to the part that influences your every move, thought and decision (unconsciously) during every waking and sleeping second and actually make it work for you?

Imagine making life shaping positive decisions even when you're asleep, and your mind and body following through because you have "rewired" your neural pathways.

Instead of going down the constant "negative" pathway that they have been used to, you are now forming much more exciting "neural" pathways to "positivity" which will only increase and get stronger every time you use them.

10. Powerful Visualisation Techniques:

The purpose of visualization is to enable you to quickly clear mental stress when your mind is racing with tension, and anxious thinking.
This visualization process, when practiced frequently, is very effective for eliminating deep-seated mental anxieties or intrusive thoughts.

There's been a lot said about this over the years and the best-selling DVD "The Secret" gave many people their first insights into the concept of creative visualisation and indeed many successful sport stars and celebrities use creative visualisation as an incredibly powerful tool to achieve their goals and aims.
The key to successful creative visualisation is not just to "see" yourself achieving something but to also experience it on every level possible so it seems that you already have what it.

Here's a link to a powerful creative visualization I've created just for you: (20-minute exercise)

There is no right or wrong way to carry out the visualization. Be intuitive with it and do not feel you are unable to carry it out if you are not very good at seeing mental imagery, as long as your attention is on the exercise, you will gain benefit.

Remember... Twenty's Plenty!

Chapter 45: Mental well-being...keep your temple water tight!

Your lifestyle tomorrow and the way you feel about yourself starts in the thoughts you are having about yourself today, as your life today and the way you feel about yourself today were created from yesterday's thoughts and actions.
Be the person you want to be from today!
These are words that I very firmly believe in and if you started to practice these very simple concepts it will make a huge difference in not only planning your life but will assist you in creating the lifestyle you've always wanted and desired and give you the self-confidence and self-esteem you've always dreamed.
To my mind and with the experience I've gained over the years working with hundreds of individuals and key UK businesses I believe these eight key points are the formula for making positive and lasting change in your life.

The myth of work-life-balance
When you say to yourself over and over "I must achieve work life balance" what is it that you are concentrating the most? That's correct, work life balance, so the very first thing that springs to mind is "work" and we all know the law of attraction clearly states that the thing we focus on the most will be the thing that manifests itself in our lives, therefore I always suggest the best thing to focus on is actually "achieving a more balanced life" that way you not only send out a much more universe friendly message but also programme your subconscious mind in the process to something that is much more achievable and pleasurable.

Are you where you want to be in your life and
If not why not and what are you doing about it?
So many people question where they are in life without actually doing anything positive about it. To make things happen you must act, remember that, simply sitting there and

thinking what a crap lot you have in life is a complete waste of time and energy. Action creates momentum, momentum creates results!

Learn how to say no
Don't accept that is given to you at work or in your life, so many people meekly take on tasks when they are already working to capacity or offer to do something for a family member because it seems the right thing to do. If it doesn't feel right or you simply cannot think of how you can manage to do it learn to say no and give a valid enough reason as to why you can't accomplish the task!
It doesn't make you a bad person or an inconsiderate person and if you're reasons are credible it will have the opposite affect to what you're thinking and make that other person look at you with a new-found respect because you set your boundaries.

Living at cause or affect
Are you one of those people who stubs your toe when you get out of bed, get up late, don't have time to eat breakfast, miss your train and get to work late then proceed to blame everything and everyone in your life for what a shitty day you're having? Welcome to the world of being a victim someone who isn't capable of taking responsibility for their own lives and what happens in it, a person living at "cause" and unwilling to recognise their own limits and misgivings. Taking responsibility for whatever happens in your life is a huge responsibility but once you accept that you are the cause of everything that happens in your life magical things begin to happen because you are in control and not circumstance.

Identifying your strengths
Knowing what you're good is invaluable and gives you the information you need to not only work to your strengths but to also identify the areas that need working. If you only do what you're good at you can become bored and stale, use your strengths to your advantage and always play to them whilst brushing up on your weak areas and become much more

rounded and capable in what you do and also increase your own self confidence in your abilities.

Goal setting
Knowing what you want and when you'd like to achieve it will give you a clarity of vision and feeling of purpose that will be the fuel that will drive your life or business forward, after all a captain of a ship or a pilot of an aeroplane wouldn't set off on a journey without an end destination and nether should you be on life's journey without a goal.

The power of self-talk
The words of your inner voice can have a powerful impact on the way you look and feel about yourself and the actions you take because of it. Be very aware of the power of influence your inner voice has and start to "listen" out for any negative words or phrases you might be using on yourself and replace them with positive words and phrases instead, you'll find it will have a marked and profound effect on the way you act, think and project yourself.
These strategies work, I know because I've used them, I still use them to this day and I've taught hundreds of others how to use them to find happiness in their lives.

The time to start making those changes is quite literally NOW!

This is the moment there is NEVER a better time, tomorrow has gone, tomorrow hasn't been created yet, but remember, the life you live TODAY was created by the thoughts, feelings and actions you had yesterday, last week, last month, last year. So, doesn't it make sense that the thoughts, feelings and actions you start to have today, tomorrow, next week, next year will shape and form your life.

Keys to an achievable outcome: (20-minute exercise)

Here is my formula for you to achieve what you wish to create in your life.

Please sit down quietly and take your time while answering the questions.

Remember… Twenty's Plenty!

Ok so now we've looked at the best of what you want to see in your future, let's take a look at turning all that theory into practical, tangible results

Begin by asking yourself: "How is it possible that I (they) don't have it now?"

1.   Stated in the positive.
        What specifically do you want?

2.   Specify present situation.
        Where are you now?

3.   Specify outcome.
        What will you see, hear, feel, etc., when you have it?

 As if it's happening now. Present tense
Make it compelling, give it some juice
Insert the picture in the future. Where is the future, in front of you? To the left, the right? Somewhere else?

4.   Specify evidence procedure.
        How will you know when you have it?

5.   Is it congruently desirable?
        What will this outcome get for you or allow you to do?

6.   Is it self-initiated and self-maintained?
        What's the first step you can take, and what can you do to keep it coming?

7.   Is it appropriately contextualized?

Where, when, how, and with whom do you want it?

8.   What resources are needed?
What do you have now, and what do you need to get your outcome?
Have you ever had or done this before?
Do you know anyone who has?
Can you act as if you have it?

9.   Is it ecological?
For what purpose do you want this?
What will you gain or lose if you have it?
□□□□□□□□□□□□□□□□□□□
What will happen when you get it?
What won't happen when you get it?
What will happen if you don't get it?
What won't happen if you don't get it?

The last four are from Cartesian Logic. They smoke out any last hidden challenges – an objection has to "prove" in all 4 segments to exist. Trust me, it's Quantum Physics – it'd take a whole book to explain that last bit alone. Just ask yourself the questions. Now by this point if you've worked a goal through the keys to an achievable outcome, you have a well formed goal at both the conscious and unconscious level.

Remember… Twenty's Plenty!

If you liked this book, please help me out and leave me a nice review on

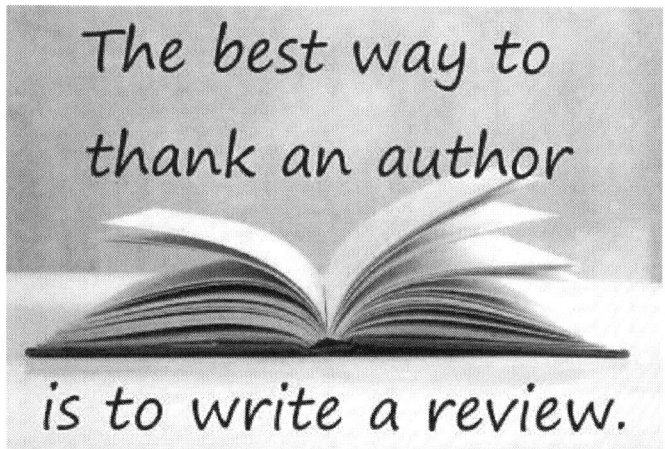

The best way to thank an author

is to write a review.

Amazon.co.uk. That helps me feed myself and my family ☺

   If you enjoyed this book then you have my permission to lend it to someone and share it with friends & colleagues

   If you devoured this book and are hungry for more, then read on – I have a special offer for you…

> *"Action Creates Momentum & Momentum Creates Results"*
> **Garth Delikan**

Stop Putting Up With Procrastination:

"Here's How You Can Easily Conquer Fear & Finally Achieve The Things You Want... *Without Pain*!"

Dear Friend,

How much is the self-satisfaction of achieving your goals worth to you?

Suppose you could take small baby steps and feel proud of yourself for stepping out of your comfort zone?

Imagine... achieving more in the next 30 days that you've achieved in the last year.

Sounds too good to be true?

Well, it isn't if you have the right tools, techniques and strategies.

125

Think about it. A lifestyle expert is the most powerful ally you could ever hire. Having the support you need when you need it. Simply put, I can get you the lifestyle you desire and feeling 20 years younger, in only 20 minutes a day.

But You Applying Those Strategies Is The Hard Part...

It usually takes people years of trial and error and can cost you a small fortune to figure out just the right combinations – or even find the motivation to do what you're dreaming about. The desire has to come for within.

But instead of staying safe [but disappointed] in your comfort zone, you have to get comfortable with being uncomfortable. Don't let your desperation stifle your aspiration! Let me help you create the life you've always wanted...

"The 20's Plenty Programme"

At last! Every life strategy you'll ever need is here.

But don't take my word for it, <u>here's what customers from all over the country are saying about this unique system</u>:

"Garth cajoles, pushes, pulls and encourages you to be the best you can be."

126

"Garth is an interesting, vibrant and exceptional individual with great knowledge and skills within the well-being and empowerment arena."

"Garth is an Amazing Man with incredible originality and innovation. Likable to a fault, his charisma is contagious enthusiasm. As a coach, friend, mentor or example of good living...I highly recommend Garth"

I know you're probably still sceptical and a bit on the conservative side, but think about this – if you keep doing the same things over and over again – you'll only succeed in getting the same results. That's why I want to let try out my proven 20 minute a day programme – <u>at a deeply discounted price</u>! (I'll tell you about my unique guarantee in a moment.)

Which Of These Powerful Secrets Could You Use To Get The Lifestyle You Deserve

- The truth about Work/Life balance

- How to plan your goals to get back on track

- Learning to say "no"

- More time to work, rest & play

- Plan your day, plan your life

- Get fascinated, not frustrated

- Staying calm enough to consider your options

- Keeping your tools sharp, plus lots more

Okay, So What's The Cost For This Incredible Resource?

Well, realize that this online programme could easily sell for hundreds of pounds. In fact if you asked a top personal growth teacher, like myself, to teach this material to you, you'd be charged in the neighbourhood of £997 - £9997, not including accommodation and travel expenses.

I currently charge a minimum of £50 per hour for one to one coaching. So at bare bones minimum you're getting thousands and thousands of pounds worth of training and support at your disposal.

But I'm not going to charge you anywhere near that amount or even my minimum project price. **In fact, your total investment for The 20's Plenty Programme is only £19.97 per month.**

So what's the catch? Why am I practically giving this resource away?

Well, it's really quite simple. I want you to have access to something that you normally wouldn't be able to tap into without paying a small fortune. The "big dog" household name gurus charge huge sums of money for cd's, membership sites and live seminars, but I want the same quality of material to be available to anyone who needs it.

3 FREE Bonuses For Ordering Now!

BONUS #1

Free Bonus Gift #1: The 20's Plenty 3 Day Detox

BONUS #2

Free Bonus Gift #2: My Top 10 Stress Management Tips

BONUS #3

Free Bonus Gift #3: The Lifestyle Guy's 10 Essential Commandments For Success

Together these 3 free bonuses are worth more than triple your investment in The 20's Plenty Programme -- but they're all yours absolutely free when you join today.

100% Risk-Free Guarantee:

Your success in using The 20's Plenty Programme is completely guaranteed. In fact, here's my 100% Better-Than-Risk-Free-Take-it-To-The-Bank Guarantee:

> **I personally guarantee that if you join the programme and study the materials, and implement them into your daily life – then you WILL see changes in only 20 minutes a day.**
>
> **HOWEVER, if after a full 30 days, you honestly believe I haven't delivered on this promise then let me know and I'll issue you a prompt and courteous refund. Plus, the free bonus gifts are yours to keep regardless, just for your trouble.**

Is that fair or what?

That means you can try out all the **The 20's Plenty Programme** at my risk, while you see if they work for you or not. And if they don't produce, I honestly want you to ask for your money back. And I'll let you keep the free bonus gifts as my way of thanking you for giving the Programme a try.

There is absolutely no risk, whatsoever on your part. The burden to deliver is entirely on me. If you don't produce immediate results using these life hacks then I'm the loser, not you.

Look at it this way -- £19.97 is really a painless drop in the bucket compared to the money you're going to waste on ineffective gym memberships, personal trainers or retail therapy this year. That's why...

You Really Can't Afford Not To Invest In This Training!

It's easy to get started right away. Just go to

https://garthdelikan.com/now-signup/

Get ready to get the lifestyle you desire and feeling 20 years younger, in only 20 minutes a day.

Sincerely,

Garth Delikan
The Lifestyle Guy

P.S. Just think! You'll never again be frightened to look at any reflection of yourself in any of the 3 mirrors – physically, emotionally and mentally.

P.P.S. In only 20 minutes a day you can have tons more energy, feel confident and strong and look like you did 20 years ago.

Printed in Great Britain
by Amazon